Unfuck Your Intimacy Workbook

USING SCIENCE FOR BETTER RELATIONSHIPS, SEX, & DATING

Faith G. Harper,
PhD, LPC-S, ACS, ACN

Microcosm Publishing
Portland, OR

UNFUCK YOUR INTIMACY WORKBOOK

Using Science for Better Relationships, Sex, & Dating

Part of the 5 Minute Therapy Series

© Dr. Faith Harper, 2019

This edition © Microcosm Publishing, 2019

First edition, first published November 2019

ISBN 978-1-62106-889-1

This is Microcosm #465

Cover and design by Joe Biel

For a catalog, write or visit:

Microcosm Publishing

2752 N Williams Ave.

Portland, OR 97227

503-799-2698

www.microcosmpublishing.com

These worksheets can be used on their own, or as a companion to **Unfuck Your Intimacy: Using Science For Better Relationships, Sex, and Dating** by Dr. Faith G. Harper.

These worksheets are free to reproduce but no more than two can be reproduced in a publication without expressed permission from the publisher.

To join the ranks of high-class stores that feature Microcosm titles, talk to your rep: In the U.S. **Como** (Atlantic), **Fujii** (Midwest), **Book Travelers West** (Pacific), **Turnaround** in Europe, **Manda/UTP** in Canada, **New South** in Australia, and **GPS** in Asia, India, Africa, and South America.

If you bought this on Amazon, I'm so sorry because you could have gotten it cheaper and supported a small, independent publisher at **Microcosm.Pub**

Global labor conditions are bad, and our roots in industrial Cleveland in the 70s and 80s made us appreciate the need to treat workers right. Therefore, our books are MADE IN THE USA and printed on post-consumer paper.

MICROCOSM · PUBLISHING

Microcosm Publishing is Portland's most diversified publishing house and distributor with a focus on the colorful, authentic, and empowering. Our books and zines have put your power in your hands since 1996, equipping readers to make positive changes in their lives and in the world around them. Microcosm emphasizes skill-building, showing hidden histories, and fostering creativity through challenging conventional publishing wisdom with books and bookettes about DIY skills, food, bicycling, gender, self-care, and social justice. What was once a distro and record label was started by Joe Biel in his bedroom and has become among the oldest independent publishing houses in Portland, OR. We are a politically moderate, centrist publisher in a world that has inched to the right for the past 80 years.

TABLE OF CONTENTS

INTRODUCTION

This workbook was created to go along with *Unfuck Your Intimacy*, which is a book of tools for improving intimacy in our relationships. If you've read that book, then you know that intimacy is about far more than sexual positions and naked shenanigans. Ultimately, it's about *vulnerability in connection*. And that's something we don't talk about enough. I wanted that book to honor the variety of ways we express ourselves sexually. And how we navigate our sexual relationships with others. That it's all so profoundly different and unique...and very, very, utterly, *normal* and human.

Unfuck Your Intimacy includes a lot of different tools that can be used by anyone to create healthier intimate relationships. If you've read it, you probably have a good idea which of those tools make the most sense to you. But if you are anything like me, you need a little structure to get shit done. So I took a bunch of those tools and reorganized them in a way to make them more step-wise. I also added in some extra worksheets that are informed by *Unfuck Your Intimacy* but include completely new information. Because I respect you spending your dollars on this book and I want you to get your money's worth. And then you get to rub it in to people who didn't get the workbook. You can be all *"What? You didn't even SEE the toxic relational strategies worksheet? How do you even human?"* But you won't actually do that, because that's totally a toxic relational strategy and now you know better, right?

For those of you who haven't read *Unfuck Your Intimacy* and maybe don't even want to? It's totally cool. You're not fucked if you are more of a doer than a reader. All these exercises stand alone and make complete sense as they are written here. All the information you need to get through them is totally included. Because nothing sucks more than being told to refer to

You will notice that some of these worksheets seem pretty intense. You aren't alone in that. I use them in my private practice and sometimes it takes weeks or months for people to get through some of them (especially the sexual history) because stuff gets activated that we have to unpack it before moving forward. If that's what happens with you, that's okay. It means you're touching on important, grown person stuff that you haven't gotten to before. Don't give up, but don't make yourself sick over it, okay? If you find yourself triggered, activated, or generally notice that more stuff has come up than you have the capacity to handle? Pause, step back, and get the support you need.

Make notes, try things out, track your progress and the like. Like the bad-ass unfuckener that you are. Remember that whoever you are and whatever you are looking to accomplish has a place here. Because this whole process is about self-discovery and what work we need to do to be as healthy as possible for ourselves, and for whatever relationships we choose to participate in.

Dr. Faith

PHYSICAL AND EMOTIONAL SAFETY

Emotional Safety Plan

I am starting this workbook with a super-practical safety plan. Not the cheesy kind full of suicide prevention hotlines, but one that everyone can use, regardless of trauma history. Most everyone can use some support in building self awareness while building intimate connection. We all have some shit from our past that can get in the way of having the kinds of healthy relationships we crave. And it doesn't have to even be past relationship shit. All kind of negative messages and self-talk can affect our intimacy...even though most everything you read on the subject treats them like two totally different issues. Which is dumb. So let's re-integrate our lives a bit.

Let's start by defining the word "trigger". It's one of those words that has been overused to the point of becoming meaningless. My middle aged ass gets grumpy and starts yelling at people to get off my lawn when it happens. Being pissed or feeling any kind of uncomfortable emotion related to your true present experience is not the same as being triggered. Someone pissing us off because they are acting like a douchecanoe is just that. An asshole who pissed us off.

Anyone with a trauma history is nodding their heads right now. Y'all know. And you know how frustrating it is to have your experience lumped in with so much bullshit and then you're called a snowflake for having a very, *very* real somatic, nervous system response based on past traumatic injury.

So back to a more accurate definition. *A trigger is something that facilitates* **reliving** *a traumatic event.* It means you are no longer in the present moment, dealing with present stimuli. It means your brain is playing the tape of whatever terrible shit happened to you in the past as a mechanism of trying to protect you in the present.

Once you start putting a formal plan into place to manage your triggers, you will notice some stuff works great, some stuff not at all, and new ideas may come up that you want to incorporate. You may also get feedback from the people you love and trust. Make any notes that you want to remember here, too.

When you are feeling the most healthy, happy, joyful, and well, what does life look like? *How do you feel? How do you interact with others? What do you like to do?*

What things have you noticed help you manage your triggers more effectively in a general sense? *For example, many people have noticed that getting a certain amount of sleep and/or exercise is very beneficial to them. Some people feel better when they eat a certain way, meditate, and pray, spend time with people they care about, or take time to enjoy hobbies that are meaningful to them. What activities work best in your wellness toolbox?*

What are some of the things from this list you can commit to doing on the regular to help you maintain equilibrium? You don't have to list 97 things. Maybe 1-3 things you aren't doing regularly right now that you know would really help.

What are some of the situations that you have come to realize are triggers for you? *These are generally not the big catastrophic things, but things that can happen on a more regular basis. For many people, this can be certain situations (like being in a crowded room or not doing well on a project), dates (like a holiday or birthday), or something they connect to in a very sensory way (like a smell or tone of voice). We may not know what all of our triggers are, and may sometimes get triggered without any idea what caused it. But if we start keeping notes when it does happen, we can often start to figure them out. This list can be a work in progress that you keep adding to over time.*

What are your early warning signs that you may be getting triggered? *What kinds of thoughts do you have? What emotions arise? What kind of behaviors do you engage in that you don't typically do?*

If you are triggered, what are the things you can do for yourself to help you manage your response to these triggers? *These are often things that you already do for your general wellness that become especially important in these situations but may also be coping skills or activities that you use when you are in tough situations. If you are looking for ideas, I wrote a whole book JUST on coping skills (creatively named Coping Skills, Microcosm Publishing, 2019)*

What do you need from others in terms of support? *While there are a lot of things that you are able to do for yourself, there may be times you need help from others, especially if you are working on your intimate relationships. Who do you trust to provide that support? How will you ask them for it?*

How will you know that you have been triggered past the point that you, and the individuals who traditionally support you, can handle? *What will you notice in terms of your behaviors? Your feelings? Your thoughts? What should you and the people who support you watch out for?*

If you are at a point at which you are not able to manage these triggers on your own, or with the assistance of the people who traditionally support you, what is the next step for you? *Do you have treatment professionals who should be contacted? Crisis lines you prefer? A hospital you prefer, if needed? What resources are available to provide additional support?*

Once your crisis has been managed, how will you know when you are feeling safe and secure again? *What does restabilization look like for you? How can you communicate that to the people who may be worried about you?*

S.T.O.P.: A Technique for Getting Back into the Present Moment

The STOP technique comes from Rob Stahl and Elisha Goldstein's work in Mindfulness Based Stress Reduction (MBSR). It is designed to help us manage stress in day to day interactions, but it is also hugely effective when used during times of intimacy when we find ourselves triggered or activated.

S — *Stop*. Rather than carrying on as if everything is fine when you are not, stop what you are doing for a moment to check back in with yourself.

T — *Take A Breath*. Seems intuitive, but it really isn't. When activated, we are far more likely to hold our breath or start breathing rapidly and shallowly. Take a deep breath, with an exhale that is longer than the inhale. This activates the body's parasympathetic system and has an immediate calming effect.

O — *Observe*. What's going on in your body? Any tension? Numbness? Just notice your somatic reactions instead of trying to disassociate from them.

P — *Proceed*. Now continue forward, regrounded in the present moment, at a level with which you are comfortable.

Body Safety Map

We have a culture of mind-body disconnect. And that's fucked up and toxic. If we aren't aware of what's going on in our bodies, how will we ever begin to understand our emotional reactions? Safe and grounded starts in the body.

Start by scanning your body to figure out which areas feel safe and secure for you and which tend to get activated when you are stressed. For example, I feel stress in my stomach; others feel it in their neck and shoulders.

Use the following color codes to mark the body map, and make notes too if you like.

Red – The places that feel high-range activated

Orange – The places that feel medium-range activated

Yellow – The places that feel low-range activated

Green – The places that feel neutral

Blue – The places that feel calm

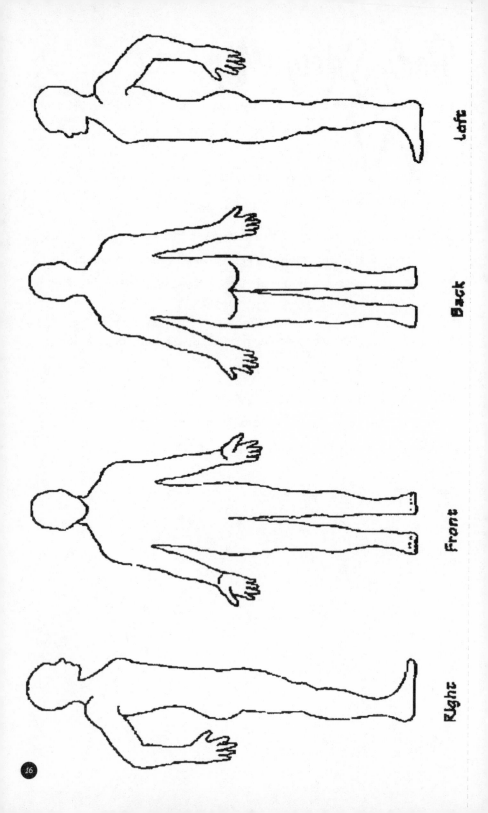

Left

Back

Front

Right

16

Where in your body do you feel it when you are anxious, angry, or upset?

Where do you feel the most calm?

This information will help you deliberately connect to your calm space, and feel calmer at times you are highly activated by intentionally stepping into your calm space until the highest level sensations are able to discharge and dissipate.

You may not be really sure where your places are, especially if you have disassociated from your bodily sensations in order to get through life without a total breakdown. That's entirely okay, and makes perfect sense. Here is your chance to start trying to connect to those sensations throughout the days and weeks ahead. You can also incorporate this work in therapy.

Once you've identified at least one place of activation and one place of safety in your body, try the pendulation exercise.

Pendulation

The previous worksheet is designed to give you a good idea of where you feel most safe in your body and where you feel most activated. Next, the pendulation exercise is designed to help you move back and forth between those sensations so you can experience feeling intense emotions without having them completely take over. Try thinking of sensations as *body feelings,* which have just as much to teach us as brain feelings.

Start with the part of your body that feels safe. This is your oasis space. For me, that's always my chest…in my heart and in my breath.

Then, move your awareness into the activated space. For me, that would be my stomach. Approach the activated space gently, with neutrality and curiosity about the experience, rather than anxiety, anger, embarrassment, and shame.

For example, you might say: *Hey there stomach, you're upset with me today. I can tell. I'm aware. Thank you for letting me know. I want you to feel safe, but you don't get to take over and be in charge.*

Then you move back to the safe space in your body. For me, that means returning to my breath.

It sounds woo-woo, but really all you're doing is teaching your brain to manage the sensations in your body. To invite the presence of your bodily sensations into consciousness without letting them go into hostile takeover mode. As you become aware of what your body is doing, you can learn to experience these same sensations without a constant sense of being overwhelmed—or even any dread of being overwhelmed.

GETTING

TO

KNOW

YOURSELF

My Relationship Values

We hear all the time about living our values. But we rarely talk about our relational values....meaning what is important to us in relationship with others. Not just to us as a unique, individual entity. Here is a chance to spend some time with that idea by identifying your relationship values and creating new commitments to living them more consciously in your relationships.

RELATIONSHIP VALUES

Make note of your top three relationship values (there's space for you to write some in if yours don't appear on this list).

SAFETY	PATIENCE	EQUALITY
RESPECT	TRUST	COMMITMENT
HONESTY	VULNERABILITY	EMPATHY
KINDNESS	SUPPORT	GROWTH
FIDELITY	HUMOR	FLEXIBILITY
STABILITY	SPONTANEITY	CREATIVITY
PEACE	CREATIVITY	OTHER
OTHER	OTHER	OTHER

Now list your top three on the next page. In the box next to the value, fill in how that value is demonstrated in practice. For example if you value "peace" as a relationship value, it may look like a quiet and tidy home that you share with a partner. Next, consider one or two ways you can better cultivate that value in your relationships. Again, if peace is your value, maybe you can cultivate it by using headphones on your laptop to watch videos when a partner is working. In the final box, consider what you can ask your partner to do that will also contribute to that value, such as carrying dirty dishes to the kitchen before going to bed rather than leaving them on the coffee table.

If your partner completed this same exercise, what did you notice about each other's choices?

Did you have any overlap?

Any epiphanies about each other?

VALUE	HOW I RECOGNIZE THAT VALUE TO APPEAR	WHAT I CAN DO TO CULTIVATE THAT VALUE	WHAT I CAN ASK A PARTNER TO DO TO CULTIVATE THAT VALUE

Sexual History

We are always telling our story. Sometimes we even use words.

Sometimes (ok, a lot of times) we have "stuff" in our history that affects our current life and relationships. Sometimes (ok, a lot of times) we aren't even very aware of what that stuff is and where it comes from. A sexual history is something that medical or therapeutic professionals may do with you if you are experiencing challenges in your sexual relationships. It helps us do a little detective work on on your possible well-hidden "stuff."

This worksheet is based on the questions that you would likely be asked if you were working with a professional taking your sexual history. In my private practice, I have some people complete a sexual history in session; many others prefer to take it home and work on it slowly on their own time and share their results with me.

Don't push yourself to complete this sexual history if you don't feel safe doing so! Some of the questions may be more anxiety-provoking than others. You do not have to answer anything that you are not comfortable exploring. However, consider that any questions that trigger a strong emotional response may be relevant to your current intimate relationships.

If issues come up that you feel require professional support, stop and contact your therapist (assuming you are already completing this workbook in conjunction with therapy). If you have been completing this workbook without the involvement of a therapist, you may want to consider starting to work with one on any of the issues that arose for you.

A sexual history should be done individually, or with your therapist, but not with your partner. You may choose to share your answers with your partner at some point, but the point of the exercise is to explore your own sexual development to gain more self-awareness of your experiences and how they impact your current self-image, relationships, and sexual functioning. What you choose to share with others (your partner, your therapist, etc.) is entirely up to you.

If you end up realizing you have a TON to write? It's totally OK to switch to a journal. You can use a cheap-o spiral bound notebook or that beautiful journal with the homemade pages that you keep putting off writing in. Chances are, there is going to be at least one question that requires you to unpack a lot. Give yourself permission to write as much as you need

Educational Experiences

What was your formal education about sex and sexuality? What classes have you had in sex and sexuality?

Was religion and/or spirituality an active part of your life growing up? How important was it to you and your family?

What was your religious background in relation to sexuality? What were you taught about sexuality in relation to your religious/spiritual beliefs and practices?

What did the adult parental figures in your life teach you or tell you about sex?

Were you allowed to ask questions about or to discuss sexual topics in your family?

How were your parents or other adult caretakers affectionate with each other or their romantic partners?

What was the attitude toward nudity (or modesty) in your home?

What did the adult parental figures in your life model about relationships and sexuality if it wasn't explicitly discussed or taught? What were their attitudes about touching? Privacy? What was their openness about discussing sexuality and relationships? Were they affirming of your sexual identity? Did they encourage exploration of sexual identity?

Did the adult parental figures in your life demonstrate emotional closeness and respect to each other? How so? To what degree?

What were your other sources of information about sex? What did you learn from siblings, friends, peers, the internet?

When did you first learn about pregnancy and childbirth? Were you given information about contraception for the prevention of pregnancy? Was the information accurate?

When did you learn about sexually transmitted diseases? When did you learn about safer sex practices about disease prevention? From whom? Was it accurate?

What was your first exposure to sexually explicit media and materials? Pornography? What materials did you see? How was it presented to you? What was your reaction?

What other media exposure did you have regarding sexuality and intimate relationships? What movies, TV shows, music, or games do you recall shaping your perceptions about sex?

Do you remember playing any games with sexual content as a child (such as "playing doctor")?

What was your first experience of nudity outside of your family or media images (i.e., locker room, slumber party, etc)? Were you a participant or observer? Was the experience positive, negative, or neutral? How did it impact your thoughts and feelings about nudity, human bodies, and sexuality?

At what age do you first recall having genital feelings? Were they enjoyable, confusing, worrisome?

What was your first exposure to differential sexual desires outside the cultural norm (homosexuality, gender variances, polyamory, fetishism, etc)? What were you exposed to? How was it presented to you? What was your reaction?

Did you have any upsetting or otherwise negative sexual experiences as a child?

Puberty and Adolescence

What would you consider your first sexual experience? Did it happen before or after the onset of puberty? What did it entail? Were your thoughts and feelings about this experience positive, negative, or neutral at the time?

At what age did you first start noticing changes in your body related to puberty? Did they surprise you or had you been prepared for them? What were your thoughts and feelings about these changes? Did you feel differently about yourself when they started occurring? Did others treat you differently?

At what age did you first experiment with masturbation (or any other solitary activity that gave you sexual pleasure? How did you learn about masturbation? How and where did you do this? How often? What were your orgasmic experiences with masturbation? What fantasies or materials did you use? How have they changed over time or have they stayed the same? What were your feelings about doing this? Were you ever discovered doing this? Did you discuss it with others?

In what other ways did you explore your own sexuality without the involvement of a partner?

What was your first orgasmic experience? What was your age? What was your reaction?

When did you first start menstruating? (If that doesn't apply to you, skip this question.) What was your preparation for the experience—were you educated ahead of time, and in what ways? What was your cognitive and emotional response to the experience? How did your parents or other adult caretakers respond? How did other important people in your life respond? How do you recall it influencing your lifestyle? Did it make you feel different about your body in any way? Did you have any menstrual difficulties?

Socially and sexually, what was high school like? Did you feel good about your body? Comfortable with your sexuality? Did others feel comfortable with how you expressed your sexuality?

What was the discourse regarding sexuality and sexual expression within your social/peer group? What was considered normal? What things were discussed? Acted on?

As you review your childhood and adolescence, what was the most negative, confusing or traumatic sexual experience that you recall?

Early Adult Sexuality

If you attended college; if you didn't, answer for that time in your life.

What was college like socially and sexually?

What were your best sexual and relationship experiences in college?

What were your most difficult or negative experiences in college?

How were your experiences as a young adult different from your experiences in high school? Were you exposed to anything new that shifted any of your perceptions? Did your values change in any way?

Partnered Sexual Relationships

At what age did you start to date in groups? Single dates? What did you most want out of dating (popularity, security, affection, sex, companionship)? Did you have the dating experience that you expected? Were your dating experiences mostly formal or informal ("friends with benefits" or "just talking" versus relationships)?

Many people engage in petting (sexual touching of the breasts or genitals while in various states of undress) before attempting intercourse. What has been your experience of petting? Where did this sexual touching usually occur?

Under what circumstances? What were your thoughts and feelings about this experience?

How old were you when you had your first orgasm with a partner? How old were you at first intercourse? Was this a positive or negative experience? How long did your first sexual relationship last? How did it end?

How have your experiences with sex, sexuality, and intimacy changed as you have gotten older? What influenced those changes the most?

What is your attitude toward sex in general? Are you content with your current sexual self? What specific activities do you find enjoyable? Do you ever feel inhibited, embarrassed, or guilty about any aspects of sex?

Have you ever had sex when you didn't want to or were not in the mood to? What was the result? What did you think and feel about the encounter afterward?

Have you ever been hurt in a sexual way or forced to have sex when you didn't want to? What was the result of that encounter? What did you think and feel about that encounter afterward?

Many people have found themselves in situations where they traded sex for money, drugs, a place to stay, or other things that they needed. Have you ever been in that situation? What did you think and feel about that experience?

Many people have found themselves in situations where they engaged in other sexualized behaviors through the course of their employment or to otherwise gain money, drugs, a place to stay, or other things that they needed. Did you ever have an experience where you used your body in such a manner (e.g., cocktail waitressing, stripping, or modeling)? What did you think and feel about that experience?

Many people have sexual fantasies that fuel their solo sex (masturbation) or partnered activity (making out, pettting, intercourse, other sexual activity). What are the themes or images that are common in your fantasies? Have they changed over time? If so, how? Are you comfortable with the content of your fantasies? If not, do you have any insight as to what triggers your discomfort? Are there any sexual acts you have fantasized about or are interested in but have not explored? Do you want to explore them or do you prefer to keep them as fantasy? If you want to explore them, what would be your ideal way of doing so? If you do not want to act on these interests, what makes that the safer choice for you?

Many people have sexual feelings and/or sexual encounters with someone of the same sex and/or gender or with someone who does not ascribe to a binary gender identity. What are your experiences in this regard? How did you react to those feelings? Were there any other consequences? What were they?

Many people have been tempted to cheat on a partner (either by violating an agreement of monogamy or violating the terms of non-monogamy). Has this happened to you? Did you follow through? How did you feel about your choice at the time? How do you feel about it in hindsight? How did it benefit or harm the relationship you were in at the time?

Many people remember seeing someone expose themselves or masturbate in public. Has this happened to you? How did you react?

Many people have unpleasant experiences involving unwanted physical intimacy with strangers, family members, or friends. Has this happened to you? How did you react?

Many people have unwanted, unexpected, or unplanned pregnancies. What were your experiences? How did you handle this and feel about it?

Many people have or have had problems with sexually transmitted infections. What is your experience?

What form of contraception do you use, if any? How consistently do you use it? Whose responsibility is contraception with your sexual partner or partners? Have you had any problems related to the type of contraception that you are using?

Many individuals experience pain or discomfort during intercourse or other sexual activities. What is your experience?

Some people have problems with frequent infections that interfere with sex, like urinary tract infections, bladder infections, or yeast infections. Have you had any of these problems?

Are there any other physical problems that limit your ability to enjoy intercourse or other sexual acts? If so, what do they include? What treatment have you sought? How have these treatments either helped or failed to help?

Any other life experiences that caused a strong or distressing emotional reaction that have limited your ability to enjoy intercourse or other sexual acts? If so, what were they? What treatment have you sought? How have these treatments either helped or failed to help?

Current Relationships (If Applicable):

Are you currently having sex with one or more people? Is your current partner (or partners) having sex with people other than you?

How often do you have sex with your current partner(s)? How often would you like to have sex? How often do you experience sexual desire (think about wanting sex, planning for sex, feeling "turned on")?

Who usually initiates sexual activity? Who would you like to initiate sexual activity? If your partner(s) is the one who initiates, how do you respond? When you initiate how does your partner(s) respond?

How much time do you spend on foreplay (touching, kissing, caressing)? On sex itself (whether it be intercourse, oral sex, manual stimulation, etc.)? Is this a satisfactory amount for you? Is there anything you want more of or less of?

Do you achieve orgasm during sexual activity? Does your partner(s)? How long does it usually take to achieve orgasm if you do? If you do not, are you able to achieve an orgasm at a different time? How are those experiences different?

When you want something from your partner(s), how do you typically let them know? When they want something from you, how do they typically let you know?

If your sex life is mostly satisfactory and you are in a relationship, what does that say about the overall quality of your relationship? What if the sex is not satisfactory? Where do your beliefs come from about the connection between sexuality and overall intimacy?

Do you feel safe in your current relationship(s)? What about these relationships makes you feel safe or unsafe?

Do you currently feel positive (+), negative (-), or neutral (=) about:

- ( ) *Your genitals*
- ( ) *Your body as a whole*
- ( ) *Masturbation*
- ( ) *Mutual masturbation*
- ( ) *Oral-genital sex*
- ( ) *Foreplay*
- ( ) *Vaginal intercourse*
- ( ) *Anal intercourse*
- ( ) *Heavy petting*
- ( ) *Manual stimulation*
- ( ) *Dry humping*
- ( ) *Orgasm through means other than intercourse*
- ( ) *Erotic media (movies, books, web content)*
- ( ) *Pornography (movies, books, web content)*
- ( ) *Sexual fantasies*
- ( ) *Your sexual orientation*
- ( ) *Your gender identity*
- ( ) *Your general sexual appetites*
- ( ) *Your general sexual activity interests and desires*
- ( ) *Others' perceptions of your sexual self*

As you look back over your personal sexual history, what would you change if you could?

As you look back over your personal sexual history, what insights have you gained into your current sexual functioning and/or intimate relationships?

What would you like to change the most about your current sex life and intimate relationships? Why are these issues the most important to you? Are they equally or more important to any current partner(s)?

Types of Touch

The idea that there are different levels of touch is a wild one to most people. It definitely isn't something that we talk about. The idea that there are five levels of touch comes from the work of clinical sexologist Dr. Patti Britton, whose work has informed mine for many years now.

Go through these questions and write down your answers. If you are partnered, consider having your partner answer these questions separately from you. Then, compare your answers.

There is no right or wrong, there is just *your* definitions. If you do this exercise with a partner and they have wildly different definitions, that's okay, too. You are discovering some really important shit about yourself and them. The point isn't to fit into a box, it's to understand our own experiences and how those impact our connections with others.

THE FIRST LEVEL OF TOUCH IS HEALING.

What does that mean to you?

What kind of touch do you consider healing?

What kind of healing touch do you enjoy receiving?

Giving?

THE SECOND LEVEL OF TOUCH IS AFFECTIONATE.

What does that mean to you?

What kind of touch do you consider affectionate?

What kind of affectionate touch do you enjoy receiving?

Giving?

THE THIRD LEVEL OF TOUCH IS SENSUAL.

What does that mean to you?

What kind of touch do you consider sensual?

What kind of sensual touch do you enjoy receiving?

Giving?

THE FOURTH LEVEL OF TOUCH IS EROTIC.

What does that mean to you?

What kind of touch do you consider erotic?

What kind of erotic touch do you enjoy receiving?

Giving?

THE FIFTH LEVEL OF TOUCH IS SEXUAL.

What does that mean to you?

What kind of touch to you consider sexual?

What kind of sexual touch do you enjoy receiving?

Giving?

Many people find, after completing this worksheet, that there are types of touch they crave that they have been missing. This is a good opportunity to make a plan to increase your intimacy in that regard. Which level of touch are you currently missing the most? What are some ways you can increase it, either with a partner or by other means?

What I Want a Partner to Know About Me

L et's face it, we all have stuff we wish that others would just intuitively understand about us. Some people are great at that intuitive-knowing business, but most of us are decidedly unfabulous. Which means we have to be brave and vulnerable (bravely vulnerable?) to share what makes us tick. This doesn't seem like the kind of conversation that starts with a worksheet, but you'd be surprised how helpful it can be to have some prompts as a starting point and a way to gather your thoughts before sharing them with a partner.

Things I want to be known for and how I want to be remembered by others:

The accomplishments that I am the most proud of include:

My heroes are:

I look up to them because:

The things I regret the most:

The one thing I would change in my life if I could:

The big thing I want to tackle next:

The things that help me feel safe and secure:

The things that activate me feeling on-edge, worried, angry, or insecure:

The things I most enjoy doing FOR you include:

The things I most enjoy doing WITH you include:

The things I most enjoy and appreciate you doing for me include:

If you're feeling the stress of personal growth, take a break and color these hearts and brains.

GETTING TO KNOW YOUR RELATIONSHIPS

Relationship Timeline

The point of this exercise is to see big-picture patterns in a specific relationship. When we are wrapped up in our day to day activities, we don't often see these patterns. Or the cause and effect of how different events impact our intimacy. Whether you are trying to make a tough choice between staying in or moving on from a current relationship, or just trying to see where the patterns of disconnection might originate, this tool is a way to gain insight.

INSTRUCTIONS:

Use one color to represent yourself. Mark off any significant life events (starting school, moving, new job, significant illness [physical or emotional], etc) that have occurred while you were with your partner.

Use a second color to represent your partner. Mark any of their significant life events.

Using a third color, mark significant events specific to the relationship itself (e.g., making it official, getting a pet together, moving in together, etc.)

Now, using *a fourth color*, shade out the periods of time where you felt that the relationship was healthy, supportive, and connected.

Finally, *with one last fifth color change*, shade out the periods of time where the relationship felt disconnected and unsupportive (e.g., there was fighting or cold shouldering).

Relationships One

Beginning

Middle

Present

Relationship Two

Beginning

Middle

Present

Relationship Three

Beginning

Middle

Present

What I Appreciate About My Partner

Does this seem like a cheesy exercise? It might. But I have found it to be hugely beneficial to my clients who complete it, especially when their relationship has been rocky. We forget to appreciate the people we love the most. And we forget to share that appreciation with them. Bonus points when you share this list: You are reinforcing things that are important to you with your partner, increasing the likelihood that they will continue to do these things (or start doing them again, if they have slacked off)!

1) Be as **concrete** as pavement when listing things. For example instead of saying "making me feel safe," say "spooning with me until I fall asleep" or "always walking between me and the curb to provide a barrier between me and traffic."

2) Be **quantitative.** How much, how long, how often?

3) Frame your statements as **positives.** Instead of saying "I like it when you don't yell" say "I like it when you speak softly and gently to me."

4) Focus as much as possible on things that they can do **regularly, if not daily.** For example, instead of the Cancun vacation you took five years ago, focus more on how they put gas in your car every week, or do the dishes every evening.

Toxic Relational Strategies

What are cognitive distortions? A thought we had that we decided to hold on to as a truth...even when it's not that true, and not that helpful. It's a story we've become attached to and act from. And it ends up causing problems. Typically when we read about cognitive distortions and common thinking errors, we are focused on the types of thought patterns that lead to a spiraling of depression and anxiety. But there are other kinds of thinking errors (and their accompanying behavioral patterns) that have just as large an impact on ourselves and an even larger impact on our relationships with others. The term **toxic relational strategies** means not just how we **think** in certain circumstances, but how we **interact** with others based on those thinking patterns.

These are behaviors everyone is capable of. Everyone has engaged in some of these strategies at some point in their lives. And we have all been victims of these strategies. Not just from perpetrators of abuse, but from otherwise good people who engaged with us in unhealthy ways because they thought that was the best way to meet their needs. The difference is in the degree in which we undertake them.

The purpose of this exercise is to look at patterns of interactions in our own lives, examining the toxic relational strategies that we were subject to as well as ones we have subjected others to. Paying attention to the bidirectional flow of these patterns is the first step in true change.

This list is based on research and training materials from multiple sources including the Safer Society Foundation, the University of Iowa, Moral Reconation Therapy, and my office partner (work wife) Brenda Martinez, who is a trauma-informed licensed professional counselor and licensed sex offender treatment provider. It is not intended to represent the totality of toxic relational patterns, but to start a conversation on how they affect your own life.

Anger as Means of Control: When we use anger to control and manipulate the behavior of others. The difference between this kind of anger and impulsive anger is that the anger response is turned off the minute we get what we want.

Employed by: ◯ Self ◯ Family of Origin ◯ Past Relationships ◯ Current Relationships

Authoritarian Dominance: When we hold rigid boundaries and expectations that things be done "our" way.

Employed by: ◯ Self ◯ Family of Origin ◯ Past Relationships ◯ Current Relationships

Belittling: When we treat others (or their feelings, concerns, point of view) as comparatively unimportant.

Employed by: ◯ Self ◯ Family of Origin ◯ Past Relationships ◯ Current Relationships

Black and White Decreeing: When we term everything in extremes ("I can never trust women," or "All men are players.")

Employed by: ◯ Self ◯ Family of Origin ◯ Past Relationships ◯ Current Relationships

Blaming: When we place blame elsewhere or insist that others are responsible for our behavior. Also could be termed a **refusal to accept responsibility.**

Employed by: ◯ Self ◯ Family of Origin ◯ Past Relationships ◯ Current Relationships

Compartmentalization of Behavior: When we compartmentalize our behavior to keep from feeling guilty, to justify our actions, or minimize the seriousness of them. ("I only cheat when out of town for work, never when I'm home")

Employed by: ◯ Self ◯ Family of Origin ◯ Past Relationships ◯ Current Relationships

Credit Seeking: When we want credit for good behavior (Okay, I forgot to pay the electric bill and the power was turned off, but don't I get credit for paying the water bill and the Netflix?) or credit for extremes not engaged in (Okay, I wrecked your car...but I could have lied about it and said someone rammed into it while I was at the grocery store) rather than accepting accountability for behavior in question.

Employed by: ◯ Self ◯ Family of Origin ◯ Past Relationships ◯ Current Relationships

Criminal Pride: Feeling a sense of identity and accomplishment from hurting others, e.g. "This is just how I am" or "This is just how I grew up."
Employed by: ◯ Self ◯ Family of Origin ◯ Past Relationships ◯ Current Relationships

Diverting: When we change the subject to something more comfortable, intentionally redirect the conversation, bring up another problem, or intentionally miss the point of the conversation at hand.
Employed by: ◯ Self ◯ Family of Origin ◯ Past Relationships ◯ Current Relationships

Entitlement: When we think someone owes us something or the world owes us something because we are special, different, or have been through more than others have.
Employed by: ◯ Self ◯ Family of Origin ◯ Past Relationships ◯ Current Relationships

Fact Stacking: When we arrange facts in a way to explain our behavior, while omitting other facts that don't work in our favor.
Employed by: ◯ Self ◯ Family of Origin ◯ Past Relationships ◯ Current Relationships

Fairness Violation: When we believe that everyone is treating us unfairly and/or when we keep a mental scorecard regarding "fairness" in the relationship.
Employed by: ◯ Self ◯ Family of Origin ◯ Past Relationships ◯ Current Relationships

Fight Instigating: When we encourage others to fight, then we stand back and watch.
Employed by: ◯ Self ◯ Family of Origin ◯ Past Relationships ◯ Current Relationships

Frequency Minimization: When we minimize the behavior based on frequency (It didn't happen five times, it was three times at most!). This is a form of **playing defense attorney.**
Employed by: ◯ Self ◯ Family of Origin ◯ Past Relationships ◯ Current Relationships

Gaslighting: When we deliberately obscure or twist facts to make others question their reality, memory, and ultimate sanity.
Employed by: ◯ Self ◯ Family of Origin ◯ Past Relationships ◯ Current Relationships

Grandiosity: When we make little things into huge, important things so we can shift the focus of attention.

Employed by: ◯ Self ◯ Family of Origin ◯ Past Relationships ◯ Current Relationships

Harm Discounting: When we insist that our actions did not cause the level of harm that others say they did ("I did it, but it is certainly not as bad as you think."). This is another form of **playing defense attorney.**

Employed by: ◯ Self ◯ Family of Origin ◯ Past Relationships ◯ Current Relationships

Helplessness: When we act incapable or helpless and unable to do things for ourselves, needing others to do them for us.

Employed by: ◯ Self ◯ Family of Origin ◯ Past Relationships ◯ Current Relationships

Impulsiveness: When we can't wait for what we want and do not want to delay our desires, and pursue these desires at the expense of others.

Employed by: ◯ Self ◯ Family of Origin ◯ Past Relationships ◯ Current Relationships

Intention Denial: When we deny our intention for harm. It may be true that we didn't intend to be hurtful or didn't plan a way to control someone else, but that doesn't lessen the impact of our behavior and it is another way of diminishing our responsibility for our actions. ("I didn't mean it" or "Things just got out of control.")

Employed by: ◯ Self ◯ Family of Origin ◯ Past Relationships ◯ Current Relationships

Justice Seeking: When we punish or control others and frame it as punitive toward others because of their behavior toward us. This is another form of **playing defense attorney.**

Employed by: ◯ Self ◯ Family of Origin ◯ Past Relationships ◯ Current Relationships

Justifying: When we justify our behavior so we don't have to take responsibility ("I wouldn't have hit you if you hadn't made me so angry).

Employed by: ◯ Self ◯ Family of Origin ◯ Past Relationships ◯ Current Relationships

Keeping Score: When we explain or **justify** behavior based on the past actions of others or ourselves ("I've always done more than you, so it's not a big deal that I didn't do what I said I would this week.")
Employed by: ◯ Self ◯ Family of Origin ◯ Past Relationships ◯ Current Relationships

Lying: When we intentionally state things that are not true, or do not include all details in an attempt to deceive.
Employed by: ◯ Self ◯ Family of Origin ◯ Past Relationships ◯ Current Relationships

Making Excuses: Similar to **justifying**, in that we use it to explain away our behavior rather than hold ourselves accountable ("I was depressed that day.")
Employed by: ◯ Self ◯ Family of Origin ◯ Past Relationships ◯ Current Relationships

Making Fools of: When we exaggerate the mistakes and weaknesses of others to intentionally demean them and lessen their voice and authority.
Employed by: ◯ Self ◯ Family of Origin ◯ Past Relationships ◯ Current Relationships

Minimizing: When we try to make a behavior seem like it has less impact on those around us ("At least I only made out with them and didn't sleep with them.")
Employed by: ◯ Self ◯ Family of Origin ◯ Past Relationships ◯ Current Relationships

Mind Reading: When we think we know what other people are thinking and make decisions based on these assumptions, rather than asking.
Employed by: ◯ Self ◯ Family of Origin ◯ Past Relationships ◯ Current Relationships

Ownership: When we feel a sense of ownership of other people, and feel entitled to control their behavior.
Employed by: ◯ Self ◯ Family of Origin ◯ Past Relationships ◯ Current Relationships

Phoniness: When we communicate and apologize insincerely, without fully taking responsibility and without intent to change (maybe just intending to stop getting caught).
Employed by: ◯ Self ◯ Family of Origin ◯ Past Relationships ◯ Current Relationships

Playing Dumb: When we act confused about a situation to avoid responsibility for our behavior, or continuously ask questions that imply we don't understand what others are communicating. ("What did I do? What's wrong with that? What do you mean by that?")

Employed by: ◯ Self ◯ Family of Origin ◯ Past Relationships ◯ Current Relationships

Projecting: When we presume what others are thinking, feeling, or doing based on what we are thinking, feeling, or doing.

Employed by: ◯ Self ◯ Family of Origin ◯ Past Relationships ◯ Current Relationships

Pushing Buttons: When we intentionally use information about another person to get them upset in order to distract from our behavior.

Employed by: ◯ Self ◯ Family of Origin ◯ Past Relationships ◯ Current Relationships

Secretive Behavior: When we hide our activities and omit information to keep people from knowing what we are doing.

Employed by: ◯ Self ◯ Family of Origin ◯ Past Relationships ◯ Current Relationships

Selfish Intent: When we think and act in terms of our needs only, and not the needs of others.

Employed by: ◯ Self ◯ Family of Origin ◯ Past Relationships ◯ Current Relationships

Self-Pitying: When we use statements decrying how bad we are in order to get attention paid to us ("No one cares about me" or "Everyone would be better off without me around")

Employed by: ◯ Self ◯ Family of Origin ◯ Past Relationships ◯ Current Relationships

Spiritual/Philosophical Bypassing: When we invoke religion or spirituality over personal responsibility in an attempt to ascribe different meaning to a situation or to avoid doing the work around uncomfortable emotions ("I'm just turning it over to God." Or "What does any of this mean at a constructivist level, anyway?")

Employed by: ◯ Self ◯ Family of Origin ◯ Past Relationships ◯ Current Relationships

Uniqueness: When we believe that we are unique in such a way that consideration of others (and sometimes rules and laws regarding conduct) do not apply to us in the same way.

Employed by: ◯ Self ◯ Family of Origin ◯ Past Relationships ◯ Current Relationships

Vagueness: When we respond vaguely or unclearly in order to distract from the truth or the content of the conversation.

Employed by: ◯ Self ◯ Family of Origin ◯ Past Relationships ◯ Current Relationships

Victimization Reversal: When we present ourselves as the victim in a scenario, rather than taking responsibility for our role in any events that occurred.

Employed by: ◯ Self ◯ Family of Origin ◯ Past Relationships ◯ Current Relationships

Wearing Down: When we continuously challenge others to give us what we want until they acquiesce out of exhaustion over the continued fighting.

Employed by: ◯ Self ◯ Family of Origin ◯ Past Relationships ◯ Current Relationships

Zero State: Feeling worthless, like nothing, a no-body, and/or empty inside and behaving in ways to help fill that void. This is often where narcissistic behavior stems from.

Employed by: ◯ Self ◯ Family of Origin ◯ Past Relationships ◯ Current Relationships

Questions to consider as you go through this list:

Did you notice any patterns in your answers? Do certain strategies come up time and again?

What strategies have you used on other people?

Do you use different strategies for different people (partners versus friends versus family, for example)?

What strategies were used against you in the past? By whom?

What strategies are being used against you in current relationships? By whom?

Are there any patterns that you notice in the strategies you use and the ones used against you?

Are there any patterns that you notice in the strategies that have been used against you in the past and are being used against you in current relationships?

What is one strategy that you have noticed in yourself that you want to commit to changing? How will you do so?

What is one strategy that you have noticed in your current relationships that you are committed to no longer accepting? How will you do so?

Spiritual Messages Kept or Released

Many people fully reject the religious upbringing of their youth as part of their healing journey. But I have had many clients report a profound sense of loss in doing so. And I think there is a middle way. I define spirituality as purposeful belonging. Embracing something that is bigger than us, that provides guidance on being better human beings, isn't a bad thing. We can embrace purposeful belonging by living in connection, compassion, and kindness. Consider taking some time to separate out the positive and negative spiritual messages of your childhood before rejecting your history entirely.

POSITIVE SPIRITUAL MESSAGES THAT CONTINUE TO GUIDE MY LIFE AND RELATIONSHIPS	RELIGIOUS MESSAGES THAT I RELEASE BECAUSE THEY DO NOT SERVE ME

POSITIVE SPIRITUAL MESSAGES THAT CONTINUE TO GUIDE MY LIFE AND RELATIONSHIPS	RELIGIOUS MESSAGES THAT I RELEASE BECAUSE THEY DO NOT SERVE ME

Reframing Toxic Self-Talk

A good chunk of *Unfuck Your Intimacy* is about problems we can have with intimacy based on our past experiences. It could be a trauma history, it could be messages that we received about sex that were prescriptive and stigmatizing. It could be our own frustrations with how our bodies operate. No matter the source, these messages start to become our inner dialogue, and the best way to combat it is to notice when it comes up and consciously reframe the messages until those new messages become our inner dialogue.

Use this worksheet to start tracking the toxic things you tell yourself. Then consider either a more accurate or at least a more balanced, helpful message. A **more accurate** message challenges the original toxic message entirely. A **more balanced, helpful** message acknowledges a fundamental truth, while focusing on managing it in a more empowering way.

Here's an example of each!

TOXIC MESSAGE	ALTERNATIVE RESPONSE	BALANCED, HELPFUL RESPONSE
Being pansexual means that I am a sinner and an affront to God.	I am a beloved child of God, made in Their image. There are many theological discussions that embrace both me and my identity and I can choose them over a message of hate.	*X*
My chronic pain makes me a terrible sexual partner.	*X*	I have to be more inventive and creative to enjoy and share my sexual self, but I am learning all kinds of strategies I can use to make sex fun for me and a partner.

TOXIC MESSAGE	ALTERNATIVE RESPONSE	BALANCED, HELPFUL RESPONSE

I Statement Worksheet

I f we taught "I statement" communication in kindergarten, I wouldn't have a job. It invokes a language of responsibility for our own emotional content, while sharing with others how their behavior has informed our emotional content.

Communicating in this way is going to feel weird and difficult at first, because it simply isn't how people discuss their emotions in this country.

My favorite story is the client I had years ago who started her I statement by saying *"I feel you're being an asshole!"* Funny as hell. Not an I statement.

Some better examples:

I feel anxious when your voice gets loud during discussions. What I want is for you to not raise your voice to me.

Extra credit for explaining the "why" of what you're feeling, like this:

I feel frustrated and hurt when you agree to do the dishes before I get home and you don't do them. What I want is for you to follow through on tasks you agreed to complete. I feel cared for when you prioritize something that is important to me and I like coming home to a clean kitchen so I can start dinner right away because I'm generally starving by then.

You can even take an extra step in acknowledging that they didn't intend the distress you felt. This can go a long way into disarming a potential fight. For instance:

I felt uncomfortable when you made that joke just now. I know you just meant it to be funny and thought I would laugh rather than be upset. But I struggle with jokes about that topic because I was bullied a lot in school about that. I would really appreciate it if you didn't tell jokes like that around me.

Try this with your partner when you are all kinds of hacked off (or all kinds of thrilled, for that matter). Here's a good chance to practice using some of the more common issues that come up for you and the people you have to communicate with on a regular basis.

I feel _____

when you _____

What I want is _____

I feel _____

when you _____

What I want is _____

I feel _____

when you _____

What I want is _____

I feel _____

when you _____

What I want is _____

I feel _____

when you _____

What I want is _____

I feel _____

when you _____

What I want is _____

I feel _____

when you _____

What I want is _____

Language Elimination

T here are certain words and phrases that are just so toxic to communication that they absolutely need to go buh-bye. Let's talk about them and what we can use instead, eh?

"Nothing/I Don't Know" :::shrug:::

Do you know when you are so upset that people can see the fumes coming off you? And they ask us what's up and we respond with one of these? It's not helpful. If you aren't sure what's wrong, it's OK to say that. Or if you want to talk about it but you don't want a huge fight, say that too. If your partner uses this language to you when you ask *them* what's wrong: don't take the bait. Communicate that you know something is up, and are ready to talk whenever they are.

What You Can Say Instead:

What You Can Say To A Partner Who Responds To You Like That:

"Whatever/I Don't Care."

When used against a partner, it's dismissive of their experience, right? When it's used about our own emotional content, it's saying I don't trust you with the truth. Both are toxic when it comes to resolving a situation. It's OK to say you are overwhelmed and are not sure how to respond if that's the case. And if you DO know and care, speak up! If your partner uses these phrases, you can kindly point out that YOU care and are trying to come up with a solution that works for the both of you.

What You Can Say Instead:

What You Can Say To A Partner Who Responds To You Like That:

"Always/Never"

Down with all binaries! Gender binaries, orientation binaries, and binary absolutes about the behaviors of others. Be specific about behaviors rather than general, and respond to general accusations with requests for specifics. Point out where things have gotten better or worse. The point is to resolve something, not scream about terribleness, right?

What You Can Say Instead:

”…but….”

But negates all good things you said before it. Every time. You did good things times a thousand…but…you forgot to take the trash out. Far better model? Good thing, good thing, something that you want to work on, finish off with good thing. And change the BUT to an AND. No matter how nice you are trying to be, brains will dismiss everything before the but!

What You Can Say Instead:

What You Can Say To A Partner Who Responds To You Like That:

"You shouldn't feel that way…"

Being told how you should feel super sucks. It's just your feelings right? Not right or wrong…just IS. And when we are using our I statements, we are taking responsibility for them. Even if they are kinda (or really) irrational. They're there. Responding with "Wow, that's really intense for you…" is far more disarming than responding with defensiveness. And if someone criticizes your feelings? Remind them that you are taking responsibility for them, not asking them to.

What You Can Say Instead:

What You Can Say To A Partner Who Responds To You Like That:

A theoretical orientation I borrow from on the regular is dialectical behavioral therapy. Developed by Marsha Linehan to help individuals with borderline personality disorder (BPD) better self regulate, it matches traditional cognitive techniques with mindfulness and distress tolerance based skills. Since developed, its been shown to be effective in many different situations. And one of the core areas that DBT focuses on is interpersonal effectiveness. That is, maintaining a clear understanding of our own boundaries, and attending to our wants and needs, while respecting the other person and the relationship itself. DBT is a skills-based approach that uses alot of acronyms to help frame the skills. One of the interpersonal effectiveness skills I use often is the THINK skill, because it is specifically designed as a tool to not only communicate effectively with a partner, but also keep from dumping a ton of negative emotions into the conversation even when upset. Like every skill, it's easier to practice using it before you're in a negative place. After awhile it will become second nature to communicate using THINK, which will make arguements far easier to manage.

T.H.I.N.K.

T stands for "**Think**." Yup, super original. But hey, the thoughtful part of our brain can shut down when we are upset. And in this case it means think of the other person's perspective on the issue. Where are they coming from? Do they see it in a different way from you?

H stands for "**Have Empathy**." Empathy is different from sympathy. It doesn't mean "feel sorry for," it means really connecting to the other person's emotional experience. Remember to connect to their emotional content, not just your own.

I stands for "**Interpret Their Behavior**." And let your imagination take over. You can start with the most irrational, ridiculous thing possible ("They totally schemed to fuck me over..it is part of their master, evil plan of world domination!") to the more reasonable. ("Their behavior wasn't thoughtful, but it wasn't intentionally hurtful.") Starting with the the most extreme seems counterintuitive, but it burns off some steam and helps connect us to how over-reactive we can be when upset..which allows us to more easily accept a rational interpretation.

N stands for "**Notice**." This means simply notice how your partner is responding and interacting. Notice when they are trying to make improvements. Notice their reaction to you. Notice the other things going on in their life that are operating as either positives or negatives. Pay attention to where they are at, not just where you are at.

K stands for "**Kindness**." Even if you are having to make a hard decision or hold firm to a boundary doesn't mean you have to be mean, right? And honestly, consistency and firmness are also a form of kindness. And you can express that in words, as well as actions. "Fuck off and leave me alone." isn't kind. But "I'm not going anywhere, and I know we will work through this but right now I need some time to calm down so we can discuss it more effectively." is kind. It maintains commitment and attachment, and expresses a needed boundary and break from a difficult situation, while taking responsibility for the need.

If you're feeling the stress of personal growth, take a break and color these brains:

Language Boundaries

We all describe ourselves in different ways and there is a huge impact on how these descriptions shape how others perceive us but how we perceive ourselves. Communicating the importance of the words that you associate with yourself to a partner is an important step in communicating who you are and what is important to you.

What are your gender descriptive words (enby, woman, queer, man, she, he, zie, they, etc)?

What are your body part descriptive words (chest, breasts, vulva, vagina, penis, dick, clit, etc)?

What are your sexual orientation descriptive words (pan, bi, gay, straight, grey, ace, demi, stone, etc.)

What are your relationship descriptive terms (significant other, person I'm dating, partner, boyfriend, girlfriend, umfriend, boo, bae, sweetie, etc.)?

What words do you find triggering, activating, or you really dislike and do not want used to describe you?

Is there anything else around language that a partner would need to know? For example, do you use different words around different people? Are there nicknames others call you that you don't want a partner using? If someone uses descriptive language that your partner knows is on your no-fly list, how do you want them to respond (correct others, let you handle it, etc.)?

Boundaries Around Sexual Consent

We would save so much time on missed opportunities and hurt feelings if we communicated this information up front, wouldn't we? This worksheet creates a solid framework around those conversations. I suggest filling out your own without a partner around and having them do the same. Then you can share your answers with them, look for overlap, and plan your menu together! A couple of notes:

1) Don't forget to notate whether you're into giving, receiving, or both. In the "no" category, you can also include off limits parts of your body (no touching of my thighs, no sex with my binder off, etc.)

2) And for the "fantasy" category, make notes on how you would be interested in engaging in sharing that fantasy if you have ideas (dirty talk, erotica, in-person roleplaing games, online roleplaying games, watching recorded porn, camming, chaturbation, going to a club, meet-up, or party either together or alone that allows viewing, etc.)

YES, PLEASE

NO, NOT RIGHT NOW

MAYBE (LET'S DISCUSS)

FANTASY PLAY

Physical Boundaries Chart

M ark positive, neutral, and no go body touch areas:

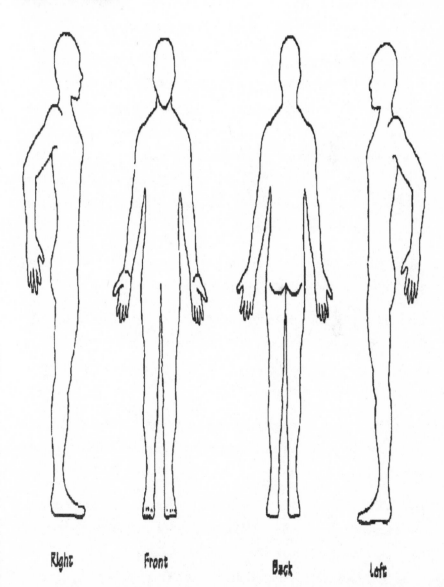

Right   Front   Back   Left

Kegels

Being healthy is far easier if we exercise, right? Sexual health has its own exercise...the kegel. Kegel exercises are designed to strengthen the pelvic floor muscles, focusing specifically on the "PC" (pubococcygeus) muscles. Kegels have tons of practical use for all kinds of issues, no matter what parts you have.

Dr. Arnold Kegel was a gynecologist who developed these exercises for women who had pelvic floor weakening post childbirth. He found another interesting side benefit: His patients who were doing kegels regularly were achieving orgasm with greater ease and frequency, and had a more intense experience, showing that kegels have an additional benefit to sexual intimacy. They have been found to help people (of all genders) better achieve orgasm, and can help all sexes feel more in control of their sexual experience for a few reasons:

Kegels help control urinary incontinence, so many individuals feel more secure during sexual activity and are less likely to leak urine.

Kegels help give the individual on the receiving end of penetrative intercourse more control over the experience and more intense orgasms. They also create a tighter vagina or anus, therefore increasing the pleasure of the penetrating partner as well.

Kegels help bring more blood flow to the pelvic region in individuals with vaginas and the perineum region in individuals with penises, potentially intensifying your arousal.

Kegels can be done with or without an aid (such as a dildo, vibrator, or tool designed specifically for kegel mastery like Betty Dodson's kegelciser). They can be done solo (which is usually a good place to start) as well as during penetrative intercourse (which can be a lot of fun for both partners).

Here's how to do them:

• Locate the muscle group in question by squeezing the muscles you use to stop your urine flow.

• If you are urinating and are able to halt the flow, you have the right muscle group.

• Your stomach and buttocks muscles should not tighten in the process. • You also don't want to do your kegel exercises when emptying your bladder on a regular basis. That can lead to weakening the pelvic floor muscles which can prevent you from fully emptying your bladder (which, in turn, can lead to an increase in urinary tract infections).

• If you are using a kegel aid, lubricate the aid before insertion and practice kegels lying down. If you are not using an aid, it may be of benefit to at first practice lying down.

• Squeeze the muscle group for three seconds, then release for three seconds.

• Complete 10 to 15 cycles of squeeze and release.

Try to do this at least three times a day. The more regularly you perform the exercise, the better results you will get (just like any exercise).

As you get more comfortable doing this, you will find that you don't have to set aside "kegel time" to be effective. You can do them while engaging in other activities since no one will know what you are up to—unless of course you are doing them during sex, in which case your partner will know and appreciate it!

Interoception Exercise

This exercise is a practice designed to build interoception. It's adapted from Peter Levine's fantastic book *In An Unspoken Voice*:

• Hold out one of your hands. It doesn't matter which one, but take note of your choice. Hold it in the air, without letting it rest against another surface (like a table top or your leg).

• Open up the palm of that hand, facing back toward your body, and use your eyes to observe it.

• Slowly make a fist with that hand, watching the whole time. Take note when your hand feels completely closed into a fist.

• Without breaking eye contact, open your hand back up.

• Now close your eyes, and repeat this exercise.

• Feel what open feels like from the inside, then the act of closing your hand into a fist, then reopening. Pay attention to all that you notice in your body that wasn't present when you were focusing on your external sight messages.

How did your awareness of the experience change once you were entirely dependent on your internal sense messages?

Was it disconcerting at any point? Comforting?

Did anything shift or feel different in how you connect with your self?

NAME YOUR SENSATIONS

Sensations and emotions are both considered "feelings" words but they aren't the same thing! Sensations are the physical ways our **bodies** feel at any given time, and emotions are what our minds feel about what is going on around us. Sensations words go along with our emotions words to help give us information. We often notice our sensations first and can use them to help us identify our emotions. For example, noticing that we are tense and hot may help us realize we are angry, while feeling jittery and shaky may help us realize we are nervous. Like emotions, sensations are designed to give us information and not last forever.

These words can be used to reclaim our language about sensation and reclaim our bodies by understanding how our thoughts and feelings are physically affecting us. Connecting to these sensations can help us better learn to manage our symptoms of stress and trauma. Often we are disconnected from our bodies and don't have a language for what we're feeling.

Check in and pay attention to your body and see if any of these words are a fit. It's okay if they aren't—that's good information to have, too.

Burning/Hot/Cold/Warm/Chilly/Icy/Cool/Clammy/Chilly/Sweaty/Gentle

Sharp/Dull/Rough/Smooth

Shaky/Trembly/Tingly/Twitchy /Butterflies/ Jittery/Jumbled/Itchy/Jumpy

Weird/Off-Kilter/Off-Center/Edgy/Tearful/Owie

Hard/Soft

Stuck/Weak

Strong/Tough

Small/Large

Sour/Sweet/Bitter/Salty/Pungent

Relaxed/Calm/Peaceful/ Flowing/Spreading/Silky/Still/Tranquil/Comfortable

Undisturbed/Chill/Still/Quiet/Peaceful

Empty/Full

Fast/Slow/Still

Tight/Tense/Pressure/Vibrating/

Dizzy/Fuzzy/Blurry/Woozy/Faint/Light-Headed

Numb/Prickly/Tickly/ Goose-Bumpy/Uncomfortable

Light/Heavy

Open/Closed/Loose/Tight

More body qualities to pay attention to: Pressure, Air Current, Pain, Tingling, Itching, Temperature, Size, Weight, Shape, Motion, Speed, Texture, Earth Element, Color, Smell, Taste, Sound, Lack of Sensation. Or add your own!

Progressive Muscle Relaxation

The purpose of this exercise is to gain awareness of how our body is operating from the inside. You know, that interoception thing I was yammering on about. Actively engaging in progressive muscle relaxation exercises effectively loosens and relaxes the muscles. By tightening a muscle and then releasing, you can feel the difference between tense and relaxed.

Make sure not to do any movements that cause pain. If any of these exercises cause discomfort, ease up or stop. Sometimes if you are very tense already, actively tensing your muscles with progressive muscle relaxation exercise will not be helpful. If this is the case, you may want to try passive progressive muscle relaxation exercises instead, meaning you just focus on relaxing parts of your body, rather than tensing and then relaxing to feel the difference.

Here is a script for the guided progressive muscle relaxation exercise. You can read it as you go or have someone read it to you:

• Find a comfortable position sitting, standing, or lying down. You can change positions any time during the exercise.

• Breathe in forcefully and deeply, and hold this breath.

• Hold it...hold it... and now release. Let all the air go out slowly, and release all the tension.

• Take another deep breath in. Hold it.... and then exhale slowly, allowing the tension to leave your body with the air.

• Now breathe even more slowly and gently... breathe in....hold....out... ...breathe in...hold...out…

• Continue to breathe slowly and gently. Allow your breathing to relax you.

• Focus on the large muscles of your legs. Tighten all your leg muscles. Now tense them even further. Hold onto this tension. Feel how tight and tense the muscles in your legs are right now. Squeeze the muscles harder, tighter...

• Continue to hold this tension. Feel the muscles wanting to give up this tension. Hold it for a few moments more.... and now relax. Let all the tension go. Feel the muscles in your legs going limp, loose, and relaxed. Notice how relaxed the muscles feel now. Feel the difference between tension and relaxation. Enjoy the pleasant feeling of relaxation in your legs.

• Now focus on the muscles in your arms. Tighten your shoulders, upper arms, lower arms, and hands. Squeeze your hands into tight fists. Tense the muscles in your arms and hands as tightly as you can.

• Squeeze harder.... harder..... hold the tension in your arms, shoulders, and hands. Feel the tension in these muscles. Hold it for a few moments more.... and now release.

• Let the muscles of your shoulders, arms, and hands relax and go limp. Feel the relaxation as your shoulders lower into a comfortable position and your hands relax at your sides. Allow the muscles in your arms to relax completely.

• Focus again on your breathing. Slow, even, regular breaths. Breathe in relaxation.... and breathe out tension..... in relaxation....and out tension....

• Continue to breathe slowly and rhythmically.

• Now focus on the muscles of your buttocks. Tighten these muscles as much as you can.

• Hold this tension..... and then release.

• Relax your muscles.

- Tighten the muscles of your back now. Feel your back tightening, pulling your shoulders back and tensing the muscles along your spine. Arch your back slightly as you tighten these muscles. Hold.... and relax.

- Let all the tension go. Feel your back comfortably relaxing into a good and healthy posture.

- Turn your attention now to the muscles of your chest and stomach. Tighten and tense these muscles. Tighten them further...hold this tension.... and release.

- Relax the muscles of your trunk.

- Finally, tighten the muscles of your face. Scrunch your eyes shut tightly, wrinkle your nose, and tighten your cheeks and chin. Hold this tension in your face.... and relax.

- Release all the tension. Feel how relaxed your face is.

- Notice all of the muscles in your body.... notice how relaxed your muscles feel. Allow any last bits of tension to drain away. Enjoy the relaxation you are experiencing.

- Notice your calm breathing.... your relaxed muscles.... Enjoy the relaxation for a few moments....

- When you are ready to return to your usual level of alertness and awareness, slowly begin to re-awaken your body. Wiggle your toes and fingers. Swing your arms gently. Shrug your shoulders. Stretch if you like.

- You may now end this progressive muscle relaxation exercise feeling calm and refreshed.

Body Image Work

CLOTHED BODY WORK

This is another activity designed to help you build your interoception and enhance your comfort and acceptance of your external, physical presentation of self.

If you are working with a partner during this activity, discuss in advance their role in the process. The important thing is that they listen to your words rather than correct anything you say about your body, especially your thoughts and feelings. We often want to tell our partners how we perceive them, and we often see them with much less criticism than they see themselves. It's hard not to say something akin to "No! I love your neck!" The point of the exercise is to share our own internal experience without fear of argument or correction.

It is also not your partner's job to ask questions or give feedback about your experience. The partner's job is to provide a supportive presence, then complete the activity with your support as well. It's amazing what you will learn about each other, if you are in a place where you feel safe enough to do this activity together.

Stand in front of a full-length mirror, wearing whatever clothing feels comfortable (as much or as little as you'd like). Take a deep breath and look at your body in its entirety for a few minutes. If this isn't something you often do, give yourself time to become accustomed to the experience.

Starting at the top of your head and moving downward, describe out loud each part of your body and the feelings you have about each part. If you are doing this activity alone, still say everything you are thinking out loud. It is amazing how much we say to ourselves that we are not aware of, because we don't give literal voice to those thoughts and feelings. When you're done, ask yourself some of these questions:

What did you notice about yourself? Did anything you notice surprise you? Did anything you found yourself saying out loud surprise you?

If you were to pick out one or two body parts/areas that you most dislike, what would these be and why? You can be present for these feelings, acknowledge them, and work to generate self-compassion for your experience.

If you were to pick out one or two body parts/areas that are your most favorite, what would they be and why?

Did your perceptions of yourself shift when you moved from looking at your entire body to focusing on parts of it at a time? If so, in what ways?

If you did this activity with a partner, please ask your partner to answer the following questions: What surprised you about your partner's experience?

Did they say anything you didn't expect?

Did you notice that they ignored any areas?

Did they express any thoughts or feelings that you weren't aware of?

NUDE BODY WORK

N ow, you are going to complete the same exercise, but without clothing.

If you are doing this exercise with a partner, undress, acknowledge the expected nervousness, and give permission to look at one another's bodies. Hold hands and look together for a couple of minutes, then take turns looking at each other's backside.

If becoming completely nude immediately, whether alone or with a partner, makes you uncomfortable, you can disrobe slowly as you complete the exercise. You can also incorporate softer lighting and soothing music if you find that helpful, but you don't want ambient music to be a distraction or have lighting so low you can't really see yourself.

Repeat the above steps, speaking all your thoughts and feelings about each part of yourself out loud (or writing them down if that feels more comfortable...I know this already feels weird!), and consider these questions:

What did you notice about yourself?

Did anything you notice surprise you?

Did anything you found yourself saying out loud that surprised you?

Was there anything different from the clothed version of this exercise?

If you were to pick out one or two body parts/areas that you most dislike, what would these be and why? Was there anything different from the clothed version of this exercise?

If you were to pick out one or two body parts/areas that are your most favorite, what would they be and why? Was there anything different from the clothed version of this exercise?

Did your perceptions of yourself shift when you moved from looking at your entire body to focusing on parts of it at a time? If so, in what ways? Was there anything different from the clothed version of this exercise?

If you did this activity with a partner, please ask your partner to answer the following questions. What surprised you about your partner's experience? Did they say anything you didn't expect? Express any thoughts or feelings that you weren't aware of? Did you notice that they skipped over any areas? Did anything different happen from the clothed version of this exercise?

Sensate Touch

Sensate touch exercises (also called sensate focus exercises) were developed by Masters and Johnson to help couples work through intimacy issues. They are included in this book as the final chapter because they are very helpful in rebuilding partner intimacy regardless of what caused the problem to begin with. I consider sensate focus exercises another relationship skill, just like date night, effective communication, and all the other shit I yammer on about.

Earlier I talked about the levels of touch: healing, sensual, erotic, and sexual. All forms of touch are important in our romantic partnerships and all help foster a sense of intimacy, and these exercises were designed to build on all four of these levels. One of the most important ways of doing that is not only improving our communication about touch, but also finding true enjoyment in both giving and receiving touch from our partners.

One of the biggest barriers to fostering intimate touch, both sexual and non-sexual, is the expectation of return demonstration. Instead, the giver should focus on the pleasure experienced in touching their partner, rather than focusing on what they get when it is "their turn." All relationships have a give and take, but except for the first pre-touch exercise here, time always should be set aside for the receiver to enjoy the experience without being expected to return the favor. Giving pleasure for its own sake to your partner can be its own intensely rewarding experience that fosters intimacy in and of itself.

There are many variations of these exercises out there. I designed my version to be both trauma-mindful and trauma-informed. But these exercises can be modified for any reason you need, okay?

GOALS OF THE EXERCISES

• To learn how we like to be touched.

• To learn how our partner likes to be touched.

• To find new ways to explore our needs and desires.

• To find new ways of receiving and giving pleasure without focusing on immediate sexual release.

• To demonstrate to ourselves and our partner a commitment to our relationship.

• To help build connection and deepen our relationship with our partner.

• To become more comfortable with our physical selves as our bodies evolve and change through childbirth, aging, and/or disability.

ESTABLISH GROUND RULES

Before you begin, it's a good idea to discuss what you hope to accomplish. It's a good idea to establish some boundaries up front:

• Determine if there are any areas that you do not want to have touched, and how you will communicate if that changes during the exercises. Consider a safe word or gesture if you are concerned that you may struggle with communicating your needs.

• Decide ahead of time if you desire to be clothed, partially clothed, or naked during the earlier stage sensate touch exercises.

• Consider how you will handle any unexpected outcomes. For example, one partner or both may become sexually aroused and want to engage in more than sensate touch. There is no rule, of course, that you cannot engage in activities other than sensate touch during your touch sessions, however neither partner should feel pressured to do so. Having a plan on how to handle those issues ahead of time will help prevent hurt feelings or unfulfilled expectations.

• Afterwards, talk about your experiences and whether or not you think the goals you set at the beginning are being achieved. Discuss the positives and negatives of each encounter. Use "I" statements to demonstrate your own accountability for your thoughts and feelings.

HOW TO DO THE EXERCISES

Once you've talked over your goals and boundaries, pick a time and place where you will feel comfortable and won't be interrupted by other people or by the telephone, TV, or other intrusions. For the sensate focus exercises, consider doing them in the morning if a male partner is the receiver, as testosterone levels are highest in the morning. Use lighting that feels comfortable to you and music if you find that soothing. If you aren't using your bed for the initial exercises (which makes sense if that's become a source of pressure), you can still use plenty of pillows and blankets to feel comfortable wherever you are.

Use lotions, oils, or a powder for the massage exercises (make sure to use one that is face friendly for the face caress, like a moisturizing cream). Some people find lotions and oils to be slimy and prefer talc or cornstarch (which doesn't clump, is cheap AF, and is probably already in your pantry). For the exercises that include genital stimulation, you may want to use a lubricant. This can be especially helpful if a partner with a vagina has issues producing enough lubrication due to menopause or other medical conditions or if a partner with a penis struggles to maintain a full erection. If you have not used lubricant before, read all the labels and test it out on a small area on your skin to make sure you do not have an allergic reaction. Remember not to use oil-based lubrication when using condoms or silicone-based lubricants when using silicone-based toys.

Alternate being the giver and the receiver. You can take turns during the same occasion or set separate times so the receiver can fully enjoy the experience, without having to return the favor after they are relaxed.

The person receiving the touch should state what feels good and what does not. Communicate this using "I" statements. "I like it when…" and "I don't like…" rather than "You shouldn't…" or "Stop that!" Positive redirection such as "I prefer…" always feels best to the giving partner. Positive feedback in general is always preferred, especially noises of appreciation when your partner does something you especially enjoy!

The giver should ask for feedback about areas of touch, pressure, and technique. One way to learn what the receiver likes is letting them guide your hand, especially at first. Consider using your non-dominant hand for times when a lighter touch is preferred. As you notice your partner's response to receiving certain types of stimulation, take time to focus on the sensations you feel as the giver. What does your partner's skin feel like? What does the part of your body touching them feel like as you move over their skin?

There is no time limit or limit to the number of sessions you spend on any exercise or stage. You can spend as much time as you want on each exercise before moving to the next one in order to establish comfort and trust. It is important that partners do not pressure each other to move forward until both are ready to do so. It can be very helpful to spend several weeks on a particular stage and exercise, incorporating a bit more of the body or areas of the body each time you practice.

Remember, the aim of these exercises is enjoyment, relaxation, connectedness, and pleasure. Focus on the journey rather than the end result.

PRE-TOUCH SHARED BREATHING EXERCISE

Sit facing each other. Maintaining eye contact, slow your breathing and focus on breathing in unison. If you don't have medical issues that disrupt your breathing patterns, try to breathe in to the count of three, hold for the count of three, and release your breath for a count of three. Focus your thoughts on loving intent toward your partner, such as "I choose you" or "I care for you."

Continue this pattern for two minutes. Two minutes will seem like a very long time the first time you try this! You can continue these exercises over time, extending the amount of time you spend in shared breathing.

Discuss the experience with your partner. What did you notice?

Did anything make you uncomfortable?

Was there anything you particularly enjoyed?

THE HAND CARESS

it in a comfortable position, facing each other. Using a lotion, oil, or powder gently rub your partner's hand. Spend 5-10 minutes on each hand (10-20 minutes total). Explore each finger, the pads of their fingers, the lines of their palms. Check in with your partner about the amount of pressure you are using. Focus your thoughts on loving intent toward your partner such as "I choose you" or "I care for you."

Discuss the experience with your partner. What did you notice?

Did anything make you uncomfortable?

Was there anything you particularly enjoyed?

THE FACE CARESS

Pick a position that is most comfortable for you. Many people find it works best if the giver is sitting and the receiver is lying flat on their back with their head resting on the giver's thighs. The giver should first rub a facial-friendly lubricant, like a moisturizing lotion, or powder like corn starch on their hands. Begin with the chin, then stroke the cheeks, temples, and forehead. Check in with your partner about the amount of pressure that you are using. Explore your partner's earlobes, and the indentation just behind the earlobes on the neck. Return to massaging the temples. This exercise should take about 10-20 minutes. Focus your thoughts on loving intent toward your partner such as "I choose you" or "I care for you."

Discuss the experience with your partner. What did you notice?

Did anything make you uncomfortable?

Was there anything you particularly enjoyed?

Sensate Body Work

Y ou may have noticed that the first exercises were more in the healing and possibly sensual domain. This is where we start to move into erotic and sexual!

STAGE ONE

L imit touching and stroking to areas of the body that are not sexually stimulating. Start with areas that feel safe for your partner and incorporate more areas on future turns. Oftentimes, individuals have the first session lying on their back, being touched only on the front of their body, where they can see everything their partner is doing. If that feels comfortable, start a later session with the receiver laying on their stomach and having you work on their neck, shoulders, back, and backs of arms and legs.

You can continue to include the hands and face, but also include feet, legs, and arms. Be careful for areas that are ticklish. Continue to focus your thoughts on loving intent toward your partner such as "I choose you" or "I care for you."

Discuss the experience with your partner. What did you notice?

Did anything make you uncomfortable?

Was there anything you particularly enjoyed?

STAGE TWO

Start with the touch you used in the first stage before moving on. During the second stage, you can include genital areas in the places you touch and stroke, but the intent at this point is not sexual arousal but sensual response.

Often during stage two, individuals find it works best to start by incorporating touch of the breasts and nipples, then touching areas around the genitals. Oral touching as well as manual touching can be introduced here (or in later stages) if both partners are comfortable with it, such as light kissing, licking, or sucking.

Continue to focus your thoughts on loving intent toward your partner such as "I choose you" or "I care for you."

Discuss the experience with your partner. What did you notice?

Did anything make you uncomfortable?

Was there anything you particularly enjoyed?

STAGE THREE

Start with the touch you used in the first two stages before moving to the third. During the third stage, include touch of the genitals with intention to arouse. Stroke the clitoris and/or gently probe the vaginal opening with a finger. Stroke the shaft of the penis, and the head of the penis (including the frenulum, which is the spot where the head and the shaft of the penis join). On either partner, this can include stroking the anus if the receiving partner has expressed a desire for you to do so.

Continue to focus your thoughts on loving intent toward your partner such as "I choose you" or "I care for you."

Discuss the experience with your partner. What did you notice?

Did anything make you uncomfortable?

Was there anything you particularly enjoyed?

FOURTH STAGE

Start with the touch you used in the first three stages before moving to the fourth. And, as with the other stages, not doing this one at all is completely fine. If penetrative intercourse, however, is something you want to include in your sex life, stage four is designed to get you there.

During the fourth stage, you can attempt vaginal or anal penetration either with a finger, penis or sexual aid, depending on your partner's preference. The extent of penetration and what you use for penetration and where you experience penetration is entirely up to you. For example, individuals with vaginas who experience vaginismus (an involuntary contraction of the muscles around the opening of the vagina) may need to start with a q-tip or a small vaginal dilator before even a finger is a tenable option.

Continue to focus your thoughts on loving intent toward your partner such as "I choose you" or "I care for you."

Discuss the experience with your partner. What did you notice?

Did anything make you uncomfortable?

Was there anything you particularly enjoyed?

These are exercises you can continue using or go back to regularly as you find them helpful.

Further Reading and Resources

Abusive Relationships

If you know (or are starting to suspect) your relationship is abusive, I hope you will consider creating a safety plan for yourself. Cover what to do if you plan to stay, or for when you decide to leave. You do not have to be living with a violent partner to need or have a safety plan. Some safety planning tools I recommend include:

- The Domestic Violence Safety Plan by Kellie Holly (www.verbalabusejournals.com) - this is the most comprehensive plan
- The National Domestic Violence Hotline Safety Planning (www.thehotline.org) - specifically includes help on planning to leave when you have pets
- Scarleteen Safety Plans (available on their website, www.scarleteen.com) - includes a separate plan to use if you don't live with your abuser
- The military has developed a safety plan specific to the needs of having a service-member partner (DD Form 2893)

Affirming, Sex-Positive Sexuality

Sex Outside the Lines: Authentic Sexuality in a Sexually Dysfunctional Culture by Chris Donaghue

Unpacks the bullshit around the stigma of sex and encourages self-discovery and self-acceptance.

Sex From Scratch: Making Your Own Relationship Rules
by Sarah Mirk

A love and dating guidebook that gleans real-life knowledge from smart people in a variety of nontraditional relationships.

BDSM, Kink, and Fet

SM 101: A Realistic Introduction by Jay Wiseman

The classic. A great overview of BDSM with good general information on getting started with exploring the lifestyle.

The Ultimate Guide to Kink: BDSM, Role Play and the Erotic Edge by Tristan Taormino

A great series of essays ranging from how-tos to think pieces about exploring power, pleasure, and human desire.

When Someone You Love Is Kinky by Dossie Easton

Very helpful for non-kinky folx who are looking to better understand and communicate with their kinky partners.

Boundaries and Consent

Learning Good Consent: Building Ethical Relationships in a Complicated World by Cindy Crabb

This compilation has fantastic information about applying boundaries and maintaining consent in real-life, sticky situations.

Ask: Building Consent Culture by Kitty Stryker

A guide to creating a culture of consent, and not just in the bedroom.

Consensuality: Navigating feminism, gender, and boundaries towards loving relationships by Helen Wildfell

A guide to creating or finding a healthy, successful relationship as well as avoiding common pitfalls.

Changing Bodies & Disabilities

The Ultimate Guide to Sex and Disability: For All of Us Who Live with Disabilities, Chronic Pain, and Illness by Miriam Kaufman, Cory Silverberg, and Fran Odette

Covers the multitude of ways disability can create obstacles to a healthy sex life along with great tips for overcoming these obstacles.

Guide To Getting It On by Paul Joannides

Recent editions of the print book have been abridged, so the chapter on sex and disability is now online for free download. Woot! But, FWIW, the book itself has great info in general.

Sexual Intelligence by Marty Klein

About communication and pragmatic expectations and the emotional work it takes to make sexual intimacy good when nobody involved in the relationship is a perfect performer. Not overtly about changing bodies but it actually totally *is* about just this topic.

Fantasies

Who's Been Sleeping in Your Head: The Secret World of Sexual Fantasies by Brett Kahr

The result of one of the largest studies ever done on sexual fantasy, with over 23,000 participants. Amazing information about what our sexual fantasies say about the nature of being human.

Tell Me What You Want: The Science of Sexual Desire and How It Can Help You Improve Your Sex Life by Justin J. Lehmiller

A researcher for The Kinsey Institute (toothbrush guy!!!) has taken his research on sexual fantasies and explored why they are super normal and how to share them with a partner to make your sex life hotter.

Masturbation

Sex For One: The Joy of Selfloving by Betty Dodson, PhD (and all things Betty Dodson and Carlin Ross)

Betty is the OG badass, a fine artist whose interest in the women's liberation movement turned her into the guru of liberated sexuality. This book was first published as *Liberating Masturbation*, because she saw our culture of shame and silence as a form of repression. Reclaimed sexuality as political liberty? That idea totally has my vote!

In Your Hands: The Everyman's Guide to Masturbation by Mark Emme

Most resources out there are intended for cis women, but Mark Emme's book is full of techniques for cis men (and would apply to other individuals with penises), including practices for extended sessions and controlling ejaculation, and information on using the foreskin.

Getting Off: A Woman's Guide To Masturbation by Jamye Waxman

Includes great descriptions of every part of the vulva and vagina.

The Clitoral Truth: The Secret World at Your Fingertips by Rebecca Chalker

Fantastic information about more than just masturbation.

Orientation Spectrum

How to Understand Your Gender by Meg-John Barker and Alex Iantaffi

A comprehensive and compassionate guide to all the ways we might identify and express ourselves around gender

Bi: Notes for a Bisexual Revolution by Shiri Eisner

A wonderful political treatise on the expanse of human sexuality. Really about all the ways we can be non-monosexual, not just bi.

You and Your Gender Identity: A Guide to Discovery by Dara Hoffman-Fox and Zinnia Jones

Dara is a clinician as well as being genderqueer, and this book is about exploration more than information. Parents of gender-questioning kiddos find this very helpful.

Asexuality: A Brief Introduction by Asexuality Archive

This is my go-to reference because it focuses on the voices and lived experience of ace individuals.

Stone Butch Blues by Les Feinberg

A classic novel bringing voice to and affirming the stone experience. Newly back in print and available for free public download.

Partnering Better

Hold Me Tight: Seven Conversations for a Lifetime of Love by Sue Johnson

A helpful book full of great ideas, though with some irritating self-help lingo, based in attachment theory.

How to Fight by Thich Nhat Hanh

This little book has great information about how mindfulness and kindness to ourselves allow us to let go of anger.

10 Lessons To Transform Your Marriage: America's Love Lab Experts Share Their Strategies for Strengthening Your Relationship by John and Julie Gottman

The Gottmans have done decades of research on relationship configurations and have developed excellent strategies for communicating more effectively with your partner.

Polyamory

The Ethical Slut, Third Edition: A Practical Guide to Polyamory, Open Relationships, and Other Freedoms in Sex and Love by Janet W. Hardy and Dossie Easton

This is the classic book of the consensual non-monogamy movement and is still the one I recommend most. It has great information about negotiating all types of polyamory. While pro-polyam, the authors do talk about exploring hot monogamy as an option when one partner is deeply uncomfortable with polyamory.

Opening Up: A Guide to Creating and Sustaining Open Relationships by Tristan Taormino

Another great look at all the different ways polyamory can be used to increase relationship satisfaction.

Pornography and Sex "Addiction"

The Myth of Sex Addiction by David J. Ley

Unpacks all the research that shows why comparing sex and porn usage to other addictions is a false equivalence.

Ethical Porn for Dicks: A Man's Guide to Responsible Viewing Pleasure by David J. Ley

A Q&A format book created to help men find ways of viewing and using porn responsibly.

The Feminist Porn Book: The Politics of Producing Pleasure by Tristan Taormino

Features essays by feminists in the porn and sex industry along with feminist porn scholars, including a lot of positive uses of porn.

Self-Compassion

Self-Compassion: The Proven Power of Being Kind to Yourself by Kristin Neff

This book was enormously eye opening for me.

The Mindful Path to Self-Compassion: Freeing Yourself from Destructive Thoughts and Emotions by Christopher K. Germer

My other favorite book on self-compassion! Neff and Germer do a bunch of work together, too.

Sensate Focus

Sensate Focus in Sex Therapy: The Illustrated Manual by Linda Weiner and Constance Avery-Clark

A manual created for professionals on walking clients through sensate focus activities, but also a great resource if you are doing the work on your own.

The Complete Idiot's Guide to Sensual Massage by Patti Britton and Helen Hodgson

Patti Britton is a well known certified sex coach and sex educator who uses many of the principles of sensate focus in this self-help sensual massage book.

Sex and Gender Confirmation

Sex Without Roles: Transcending Gender by Eli Sachse

A zine about exploring your sexuality in a healthy way as you transition.

Trans Bodies, Trans Selves by Laura Erickson-Schroth

This comprehensive book has a whole chapter on intimate relationships.

The Trans Partner Handbook: A Guide For When Your Partner Transitions by Jo Green

Covers a ton of different topics related to partner transition, including possible changes to sex and sexuality.

Sex Toys/Sex Aids

The Big Book of Sex Toys: From Vibrators and Dildos to Swings and Slings--Playful and Kinky Bedside Accessories That Make Your Sex Life Amazing by Tristan Taormino

Tons of information for solo and partnered use plus photos to take the guesswork of how to actually make everything work!

The Many Joys of Sex Toys: The Ultimate How-to Handbook for Couples and Singles by Anne Semans

Another illustrated guide that covers toys and toy usage techniques. Think of it as a sex cookbook with the toys as the ingredients!

Oh Joy, Sex Toy by Erica Moen and Matthew Nolan

A webcomic and four (so far!) book volumes that cover all kinds of ways of having sex, solo and partnered, for all kinds of different bodies.

Sex While Parenting

Hump: True Tales of Sex After Kids by Kimberly Ford

A collection of honest essays about reclaiming sex after having children, including stories from a wide variety of couples.

The Mother's Guide to Sex: Enjoying Your Sexuality Through All Stages of Motherhood by Anne Semans and Cathy Winks

Lots of anecdotes and tips to draw from...whether your kids are 18 months or 18 years old!

Sex-Positive Parenting

Not Your Mother's Meatloaf: A Sex Education Comic Book by Saiya Miller and Liza Bley

Comics for youth that take away the shame and secretiveness of sex education without being dry and boring. This was the book I left sitting out for my own kids!

Woke Parenting by Bonnie Scott and Faith Harper

This zine did so well that it will soon become a book. All of us next-generation parents are desperate for materials that speak to our values and the modern world. How our children express themselves, their identities, and their bodies is a huge part of that.

Sexual Abuse

Things That Help by Cindy Crabb

Cindy's second zine compilation is some of my favorite writing about healing after sexual trauma, written by an incredibly articulate survivor. More at www.dorisdorisdoris.com.

Dear Sister: Letters From Survivors of Sexual Violence by Lisa Factora-Borchers

The letters are affirming and honest without veering off into being tragedy porn.

The Sexual Healing Journey: A Guide For The Survivors of Sexual Abuse by Wendy Maltz

A step by step guide on managing your trauma responses during sexual intimacy in order to reclaim a healthy, fulfilling sex life.

Spirituality

Sex, God, and the Conservative Church: Erasing Shame from Sexual Intimacy by Tina Schermer Sellers

A dense book meant for clinicians. But it has a brilliant history of Western culture and the lens of conservative religion and how that has impacted human sexuality with ideas on how to heal from the negative messages without giving up your faith tradition.

UnClobber: Rethinking Our Misuse of the Bible on Homosexuality by Colby Martin

My absolute favorite book ever on unpacking the "clobber" passages from the bible that are used to proclaim homosexuality as a sin. By an evangelical preacher whose story of coming to allyship is as important as his scriptural interpretation.

Trauma

Unfuck Your Brain by Faith Harper

I've distilled a lot of information about the physiological underpinnings of trauma and showed you how to work with it.

Waking The Tiger by Peter Levine

A great book on how the body holds trauma and how that impacts all domains of our lives.

References

"5 Reasons People Choose to Stay Single." *Psychology Today,* Sussex Publishers, www.psychologytoday.com/us/blog/me-we/201309/5-reasons-people-choose-stay-single.

Addington, D. (1997). *A hand in the bush*. San Francisco, CA: Greenery Press.

Addington, D. (2006). *Play piercing*. San Francisco, Calif.: Greenery.

Alman, I. (1993). *Let's talk sex*. Freedom, CA: Crossing Press.

Apps, A. (n.d.). *Intersex*.

arXiv, Emerging Technology from the. "The Way Strangers Meet via Dating Websites Is Changing Society in Unexpected Ways, Say Researchers." *MIT Technology Review, MIT Technology Review,* 10 Oct. 2017, www.technologyreview.com/s/609091/first-evidence-that-online-dating-is-changing-the-nature-of-society/.

Asexuality Archive. (2012). *Asexuality: A brief introduction*.

Barker, M. and Hancock, J. (n.d.). *Enjoy sex*.

Barker, M. and Scheele, J. (2016). *Queer*. London: Icon Books Ltd.

Barnes-Svarney, P. (2012). *Why Do Women Crave More Sex in the Summer?*. Penguin Group (USA) Incorporated.

Bass, E. and Davis, L. (1992). *The courage to heal*. New York: HarperPerennial.

Becker, G. (1997). *The gift of fear*. Boston: Little, Brown and Company.

Belge, K. and Bieschke, M. (2012). *Queer*. San Francisco, Calif.: Zest.

Berkowitz, E. (2013). *Sex and punishment*. Berkeley, Calif.: Counterpoint.

Bernstein, R. (2009). *The East, the West, and sex*. New York: Vintage Books.

Binaohan, B. (2014). *Decolonizing Trans/Gender 101*. biyuti publishing.

Blank, H. (2000). *Big big love*. Emeryville, CA: Greenery Press.

Blank, J. and Corinne, T. (2011). *Femalia*. San Francisco, CA: Last Gasp.

Blank, J. and Whidden, A. (2000). *Good vibrations*. San Francisco, Calif.: Down There Press.

Blue, V. (2006). *The adventurous couple's guide to sex toys*. San Francisco, Calif.: Cleis Press.

Blum, D. (2014). *Sex on the brain*. New York: Penguin Books.

Blume, E. (1998). *Secret survivors*. New York: Ballantine Books.

Bongiovanni, A., Jimerson, T., Crank! and Yarwood, A. (n.d.). *A quick & easy guide to they/them pronouns*.

Bornstein, K. (1220). *A queer and pleasant danger*. Boston, Mass: Beacon.

Bornstein, K. (2013). *Gender Outlaw*. Hoboken: Taylor and Francis.

Bornstein, K. and Bergman, S. (2010). *Gender outlaws*. Berkeley, CA: Seal Press.

Boyd, H. (2007). *She's not the man I married*. New York: Seal Press.

Breaking silence. (1995). New York: Xanthus Press.

Britton, P. and Lerma, H. (2003). *The complete idiot's guide to sensual massage illustrated*. Indianapolis, Ind.: Alpha.

Britton, P. (n.d.). *The art of sex coaching*.

Brody, M. (n.d.). *Stop the fight!*.

Campbell, D. "Body image concerns more men than women, research finds." *The Guardian* Jan. 6, 2012. https://www.theguardian.com/lifeandstyle/2012/jan/06/body-image-concerns-men-more-than-women

Carnes, P. (1989). *Contrary to love*. Minneapolis: CompCare.

Carnes, P. (1992). *Don't call it love*. New York: Bantam.

Carnes, P. (2001). *Facing the shadow*. Wickenburg, AZ: Gentle Path.

Carnes, P. and Carnes, P. (2001). *Out of the shadows*. Center City, MN: Hazelden Information & Edu.

Carnes, P. and Moriarity, J. (1997). *Sexual anorexia*. Center City (Minn.): Hazelden.

Carnes, P., Delmonico, D. and Griffin, E. (2008). *In the shadows of the net*. Center City, Minn.: Hazelden.

Castelman, Michael. "How much of porn depicts violence against women?" Psychology Today, June 15, 2016. https://www.psychologytoday.com/us/blog/all-about-sex/201606/how-much-porn-depicts-violence-against-women

Chodorow, N. (n.d.). *Femininities, masculinities, sexualities*.

Cockrill, K., Gimeno, L. and Herold, S. (2015). *Untold stories*. North Charleston: CreateSpace Independent Publishing Platform.

Cohen Greene, C. and Garano, L. (n.d.). *An intimate life*.

Corinna, H. (2007). *S.E.X.*. New York: Da Capo.

Cottrell, S. (2014). *Mom, I'm gay*. [Place of publication not identified]: Freedhearts.

Davis, L. (1991). *Allies in healing*. New York, N.Y.: HarperPerennial.

Davis, L. (1991). *The courage to heal workbook*. New York, N.Y.: Harper & Row.

Diamond, L. (2009). *Sexual fluidity*. Cambridge, Mass.: Harvard University Press.

Diamond, M. (2011). *Trans/love*. San Francisco: Manic D Press.

Dodson, B. (1996). *Sex for one*. New York: Crown Trade Paperbacks.

Dohrenwend, A. (2012). *Coming around*. Far Hills, N.J.: New Horizon Press.

Dreisbach, S. "Shocking body image news" *Glamour*, Feb 2, 2011. https://www.glamour.com/story/shocking-body-image-news-97-percent-of-women-will-be-cruel-to-their-bodies-today

Duron, L. (2013). *Raising my rainbow*. New York: Broadway Books.

Durve, A. (2012). *The power to break free workbook*. [United States]: Power Press LLC.

Easton, D. and Hardy, J. (2004). *Radical ecstasy*. Oakland, Calif.: Greenery Press.

Easton, D. and Liszt, C. (n.d.). *The ethical slut*.

Easton, D., Hardy, J. and Easton, D. (2003). *The new topping book*. Oakland, CA: Greenery Press.

Easton, D., Liszt, C. and Beck, A. (1997). *The bottoming book, or, how to get terrible things done to you by wonderful people*. [Place of publication not identified]: Greenery.

Ehrensaft, D. (n.d.). *The gender creative child*.

Eisner, S. (n.d.). *Bi*.

Emberley, M. and Harris, R. (2009). *It's Perfectly Normal*. Somerville: Candlewick Press.

Emerson, D. (n.d.). *Trauma-sensitive yoga in therapy*.

Emme, M. (2013). *In your hands*. Berlin: Bruno Gmander.

Erickson-Schroth, L. (n.d.). *Trans bodies, trans selves*.

Evans, P. (2003). *Verbal abuse survivors speak out*. Holbrook, Mass.: Adams Media.

Factora-Borchers, L. and Simmons, A. (n.d.). *Dear sister*.

Feinberg, L. (2005). *Transgender warriors*. Boston, Mass: Beacon Press.

Feinberg, L. (2006). *Drag king dreams*. New York: Carroll & Graf Publishers.

Feinberg, L. (2007). *Trans liberation*. Boston, Mass: Beacon Press.

Fernbach, A. (2003). *Fantasies of fetishism*. New Brunswick, NJ [u.a.]: Rutgers Univ. Press.

Fields, R. Douglas (2015) *Why we snap*. New York: Dutton.

Fincham, F., Fernandes, L. and Humphreys, K. (1993). *Communicating in relationships*. Champaign, IL: Research Press.

Finley, K. (2000). *A different kind of intimacy*. New York: Thunder's Mouth Press.

Ford, J. (1997). *Child of the universe*. [Ellsworth, Me.]: [Epigrammata Press].

Forssberg, M. and Lundin, M. (2007). *Sex for guys*. Toronto [Ont.]: Groundwood Books.

Garbacik, J. and Lewis, J. (n.d.). *Gender & sexuality for beginners*.

Germer, C. (2009). *The mindful path to self-compassion*. New York: Guilford Press.

Glasser, W. (1995). *Staying together*. New York: HarperCollins.

Glenum, L. (2010). *Gurlesque*. Philadelphia, PA: Saturnalia Books.

Goad, J. (2007). *Jim Goad's gigantic book of sex*. Los Angeles, Calif.: Feral House.

Goldberg, S. and Brushwood Rose, C. (2009). *And Baby Makes More: Known Donors, Queer Parents, and Our Unexpected Families*. Insomniac Press.

Gottman, J., Gottman, J. and DeClaire, J. (n.d.). *Ten lessons to transform your marriage*.

Haberman, H. (n.d.). *Family jewels - a guide to male genital play and torment*.

Haines, S. (1999). *The survivor's guide to sex*. San Francisco: Cleis Press.

Hardy, J. (2006). *21st century kinkycrafts*. San Francisco, Calif.: Greenery.

Hasler, N. and Capozzola, M. (n.d.). *Sex*.

Heath, H. and White, I. (2002). *The challenge of sexuality in health care*. Osney Mead, Oxford: Blackwell Science.

Helminiak, D. (n.d.). *What the Bible really says about homosexuality*.

Henderson, E. and Armstrong, N. (n.d.). *100 questions you'd never ask your parents*.

Herek, G. (1998). *Stigma and sexual orientation*. London: SAGE.

Hills, R. (n.d.). *The sex myth*.

Hitt, S. (1997). *Cooking with less salt, less sugar, less fat ... in less time*. [Place of publication not identified]: Windmore Writers.

Hoffman-Fox, D., Jones, Z., Finch, S. and Keig, Z. (n.d.). *You and your gender identity*.

Hogan, S. (2003). *Gender issues in art therapy*. London: Jessica Kingsley Pub.

Holly, K. (n.d.). *Domestic violence safety plan*.

Hochschild, Arlie Russell. *The Managed Heart: Commercialization of Human Feeling*. University of California Press, 2012.

Jarvis, C. (2002). *The marriage sabbatical: the journey that brings you home*. Broadway Books/Jan.

Joannides, P., Gross, D. and Johnson, T. (n.d.). *Guide to getting it on*.

Johnson, S. (n.d.). *Hold me tight*.

Judson, O. (2003). *Dr. Tatiana's sex advice to all creation*. Metropolitan Owl Book.

Kahr, B. and Kahr, B. (2009). *Who's been sleeping in your head*. New York: Basic Books.

Karahassan, Philip. "How Technology Is Changing Dating." *PsychAlive,* 13 Sept. 2017, www.psychalive.org/how-technology-is-changing-dating/.

Kaufman, M., Silverberg, C. and Odette, F. (2010). *The ultimate guide to sex and disability*. [Place of publication not identified]: Read How You Want.

Keel, P. (2000). *All about us*. New York: Broadway Books.

Kendrick, S., Kendrick, A. and Kimbrough, L. (2008). *The love dare*. Nashville, Tenn.: B & H Publishing Group.

Kerner, I. (2008). *Passionista*. New York: William Morrow.

Kerner, I. and Rinna, L. (2014). *The big, fun, sexy sex book*. New York: Gallery Books.

Kerner, I. (n.d.). *She comes first*.

Killermann, S. (2013). *The social justice advocate's handbook*. Austin, Tx.: Impetus Books.

Komisaruk, B. (2010). *The orgasm answer guide*. Baltimore: Johns Hopkins University Press.

Kort, J. (n.d.). *Gay affirmative therapy for the straight clinician*.

Kramer, P. (1997). *Should you leave?*. New York: Scribner.

Kuklin, S. (2015). *Beyond magenta*. Somerville: Candlewick Press.

Lee, J. (n.d.). *Coming out like a porn star*.

Lee, J. (n.d.). *Torn*.

Leiblum, S. and Rosen, R. (2000). *Principles and practice of sex therapy*. New York: Guilford Press.

Leman, K. (n.d.). *Sheet music*.

Lerner, H. (1990). *The dance of intimacy*. New York, N.Y.: Harper Perennial.

Ley, D. (n.d.). *The myth of sex addiction*.

Lindner, Matt. "Does Using Social Media Make You More Likely to Cheat?" *Chicagotribune.com*, 11 Nov. 2016, www.chicagotribune.com/lifestyles/sc-social-media-cheating-family-1115-20161111-story.html.

Linssen, L. and Wik, S. (2010). *Love unlimited*. Forres, Scotland: Findhorn Press.

Lotney, K. (2000). *The ultimate guide to strap-on sex*. San Francisco, Calif.: Cleis.

Love, P. and Robinson, J. (1995). *Hot monogamy*. New York: Plume.

Maltz, W. (2001). *The sexual healing journey*. New York: HarperCollins World.

Marr, L. (2007). *Sexually transmitted diseases*. Baltimore: Johns Hopkins University Press.

Martin, C. (n.d.). *Unclobber*.

Masters, P. (2001). *Look into my eyes*. San Francisco, Calif.: Greenery Press.

Masters, P. (2007). *The Control Book*. Rinella Editorial Services.

Matik, W. (2002). *Redefining our relationships*. Oakland, CA: HMPH! Press.

Maxfield, G. (1998). *The Novel approach to sexuality and disability*. Sparks, Nev.: Northern Nevada Amputee Support Group.

Mazza, J. (2001). *Exploring your sexual self*. Cincinnati, OH: Walking Stick Press.

McCarthy, B. (n.d.). *Sex made simple*.

McKay, M., Fanning, P. and Paleg, K. (1996). *Couple skills*. Oakland, Calif.: New Harbinger Publ.

Melton, G. (2016). *Love warrior*. [Place of publication not identified]: Flatiron Books.

Merck, M. (1993). *Perversions*. London: Virago.

Mirk, S. (n.d.). *Sex from scratch*.

Moon, A. (n.d.). *Bad dyke*.

Moser, C. and Hardy, J. (2002). *Sex disasters, and how to survive them*. San Francisco, Calif.: Greenery Press.

Nagoski, E. (n.d.). *Come as you are*.

Neff, K. (2011). *Self-compassion*. New York: HarperCollins.

Northrup, C., Schwartz, P. and Witte, J. (2012). *The normal bar*. New York: Crown Archetype.

Oliver, G. and Oliver, C. (2007). *Mad about us*. Minneapolis, Minn.: Bethany House Publishers.

Our bodies, ourselves. (2008). New York: Touchstone Book/Simon & Schuster.

Parker-Pope, Tara. "More People Appear to Be Cheating on Their Spouses, Studies Find." *The New York Times*, *The New York Times*, 27 Oct. 2008, www.nytimes.com/2008/10/28/health/28well.html.

Pascoe, C. (2012). *Dude, you're a fag*. Berkeley, Calif.: University of California Press.

"Path to Safety - National Domestic Violence Hotline." The National Domestic Violence Hotline, www.thehotline.org/help/path-to-safety/.

Prooyen, Eva Van. "This One Thing Is the Biggest Predictor of Divorce." *The Gottman Institute*, The Gottman Institute 4 Min Read 10,856 The Meaning of Life Is to Make Other People's Lives More Meaningful. 15 Feb. 2018, www.gottman.com/blog/this-one-thing-is-the-biggest-predictor-of-divorce/

Queen, C. (2009). *Exhibitionism for the shy*. Gardena, Calif.: Down There Press.

Richo, D. (2005). *The five things we cannot change*. Boston, Mass.: Shambhala.

Robnoxious (n.d.). *Alive with vigor*.

Ross, C. and Dodson, B. (n.d.). *Betty Dodson bodysex basics*.

Rubel, R. (2007). *Master/slave relations*. Las Vegas, Nev.: Nazca Plains.

"Safety Planning for Domestic Violence and Abuse Victims." Abusive Relationships, Verbal Abuse in Marriage and Domestic Violence, Verbal Abuse Journals, verbalabusejournals.com/how-stop-abuse/safety-planning/.

"Safety Plan: When You Live With the Abuse." Scarleteen, 22 Apr. 2014, www.scarleteen.com/safety_plan_when_you_live_with_the_abuse.

Salmansohn, K. and Krauss, T. (2002). *The clitourist*. New York: Universe.

Savage, D. and Miller, T. (n.d.). *It gets better*.

Semans, A. and Winks, C. (2001). *The mother's guide to sex*. New York: Three Rivers Press.

Sewell, J. (2007). *I'd rather eat chocolate*. New York: Broadway Books.

Sex. (2014). Quiver.

Smith, R., Gingrich, C. and Taylor, G. (n.d.). *Speaking out*.

Sprinkle, A. (2005). *Dr. Sprinkle's spectacular sex*. New York: Jeremy P. Tarcher/Penguin.

Stahl, B. and Goldstein, E. (2010). *A mindfulness-based stress reduction workbook*. Oakland, Calif.: New Harbinger Publications.

Stern, D. (n.d.). *Swingland*.

Stewart, E. and Spencer, P. (2002). *The V book*. New York: Bantam Books.

Strayed, C. (n.d.). *Tiny beautiful things*.

Strict, M. (2003). *Intimate invasions*. San Francisco, Calif.: Greenery.

Stryker, S. (2008). *Transgender history*. Berkeley, Calif.: Seal Press.

Sukel, K. (2014). *This is your brain on sex*. [Place of publication not identified]: Free Press.

Taormino, T. (1998). *The ultimate guide to anal sex for women*. San Francisco, Calif.: Cleis Press.

Taormino, T. (2007). *Opening up*. San Francisco, Calif.: Cleis.

Taormino, T. (2009). *The anal sex positions guide*. Beverly, MA: Quiver.

Taormino, T. (2010). *The big book of sex toys*. Gloucester, Mass.: Quiver.

Taormino, T. (n.d.). *New sex*.

Tempest. (2006). *The toybag guide to medical play*. San Francisco, Calif.: Greenery.`

The "go ask Alice" book of answers. (1998). New York: H. Holt.

Tilsen, J. (2013). *Therapeutic conversations with queer youth*. Lanham: Jason Aronson.

"Tinder: Swiping Self Esteem?" ScienceDaily, ScienceDaily, 4 Aug. 2016, www.sciencedaily.com/releases/2016/08/160804172410.htm.

Tipping, C. (1997). *Radical forgiveness*. Atlanta, GA: GOLDENeight Publishers.

Two Knotty Boys. and Utley, L. (2008). *Showing you the ropes*. San Francisco, Calif.: Green Candy.

Varrin, C. (2005). *Female dominance*. New York: Citadel.

Verdolin, J. (n.d.). *Wild connection*.

Waxman, J. (2007). *Getting off*. Emeryville, CA: Seal Press.

Westheimer, R. and Lehu, P. (2009). *Dr. Ruth's top 10 secrets for great sex*. San Francisco: Jossey-Bass.

"White Mountain Waldorf School." *White Mountain Waldorf*, www.whitemountainwaldorf.org/articles/touch/.

Wiest, Brianna. "14 Perfectly Good Reasons To Not Be Dating Anyone." Bustle, Bustle, 25 Apr. 2018, www.bustle.com/articles/77335-14-perfectly-good-reasons-to-not-date-anyone-right-now-because-you-should-never-have-to.

Wijsmeijer, AA. and van Assen, MA. "Psychological characteristics of BDSM participants." J Sex Med. 2013 Aug;10(8):1943-52

Winks, C. (1999). *The g-spot*. [Place of publication not identified]: Down There.

Wiseman, J. (2000). *Jay Wiseman's erotic bondage handbook*. Emeryville, CA: Greenery Press.

Yoe, C. (n.d.). *The best of Sexology*.

SCARCITY THINKING

"There will never be enough"

Competes

Hoards

Won't share information

Doesn't offer help

Resents competition

ABUNDANCE THINKING

"There will always be more"

Collaborates

Generous

Freely offers help and information

Trusts and builds rapport

Embraces competition

Strives to grow

The best is yet to come

Sees that the pie is growing

Thinks big

Embraces risk

Takes ownership of change

Afraid of being replaced

Believes times are tough

Believes that the pie is disappearing

Thinks small

Avoids risk

Fears change

Suspicious of others

COMMON BRAIN TRAPS

Cognitive distortions are ways that our mind convinces us of something that isn't true. These irrational thoughts are a common cause of maladaptive coping and toxic behaviors, used to reinforce negative thinking or emotions. We send ourselves bad data and convince ourselves that it's true. Then they keep us feeling bad about ourselves.

Always Being Right: You must constantly "prove" yourself to be correct even when it hurts others' feelings.

Blaming: You can't see your own problems, influence, or contributions. Everything is someone else's fault.

Disqualifying the Positive: You dismiss every inch of praise as undeserved, an attempt at flattery, or naïveté.

Emotional Reasoning: You believe that negative feelings expose the "true" nature of things and that reality is a reflection of emotionally linked thoughts.

Fallacy of Change: You wait on social power structures to force someone else to do what you want.

Fallacy of Fairness: You find others guilty when they don't follow your code of justice.

Filtering: You exclude information that does not conform to your already held beliefs and focus entirely on the negative.

Jumping to Conclusions: You make negative assumptions with little or no evidence.

Mind Reading: You "know" that others must be thinking the worst possible things about you so you find no point in trying in making effort.

Labeling and Mislabeling: You judge someone's entire character and on a single mistake as judge and through your own values.

Catastrophizing: You expect that unlikely, worst possible outcomes will come true.

Magnification and Minimization: You make mountains out of molehills or vice versa.

Overgeneralization: You make broad judgments hastily without sufficient data. Every single event implies consistency.

Personalization: You put responsibility on someone (often yourself) who had no control over the events in question.

Should Statements: You believe that the same rules always create the same outcomes; no other factors should ever influence any experience.

Dichotomous Reasoning: You believe that everything is "Always, Every, or Never." When someone that you admired makes a mistake, you now have contempt for them.

Faith G. Harper, PhD, LPC-S, ACS, ACN is a bad-ass, funny lady with a PhD. She's a licensed professional counselor, board supervisor, certified sexologist, and applied clinical nutritionist with a private practice and consulting business in San Antonio, TX. She has been an adjunct professor and a TEDx presenter, and proudly identifies as a woman of color and uppity intersectional feminist. She is the author of the book *Unf*ck Your Brain* and many other popular zines and books on subjects such as anxiety, depression, and grief. She is available as a public speaker and for corporate and clinical trainings.